Absorbing the Wisdom

HOW TO LIVE
WISELY & WELL

MICHAEL E.
BRUNNER

Copyright © 2020 Michael E. Brunner
All rights reserved.
ISBN: 9780578832258

Unless otherwise noted, all scripture quotations are from THE HOLY BIBLE, NEW INTERNATIONAL VERSION®, NIV® Copyright © 1973, 1978, 1984, 2011 by Biblica, Inc.® Used by permission. All rights reserved worldwide.

Scripture quotations marked NASB are taken from the (NASB®) New American Standard Bible®, Copyright © 1960, 1971, 1977, 1995, by The Lockman Foundation. Used by permission. All rights reserved. www.lockman.org.

Scripture quotations marked MSG are taken from *THE MESSAGE*, copyright © 1993, 2002, 2018 by Eugene H. Peterson. Used by permission of NavPress. All rights reserved. Represented by Tyndale House Publishers, Inc.

Cover Design: Meghan R. Ward

"In a good bookroom you feel in some mysterious way that you are absorbing the wisdom contained in all the books through your skin, without even opening them."

MARK TWAIN

"Oh! Teach us to live well! Teach us to live wisely and well!"

PSALM 90:12 (MSG)

This little book is a distillation of the wisdom I have absorbed from others and put into practice in my life. I am indebted to all who shared their wisdom, both named and unnamed.

TABLE OF CONTENTS

ACKNOWLEDGMENTS i
PREFACE iii
SECTION 1: Elevate Your Habits 1
    Chapter 1: Developing Excellent Habits 3
    Chapter 2: Using the Mini Habit Approach 9
    Chapter 3: Implementing 11
SECTION II: Own Your Life 15
    Chapter 4: Designing Your Ideal Life 17
    Chapter 5: Taking Responsibility 21
    Chapter 6: Living Near Your Ideal Busyness Level 25
    Chapter 7: Being Positive, Optimistic, and Happy 27
    Chapter 8: Employing Positive Self Talk 31
    Chapter 9: Following the 80-20 Rule 35
SECTION III: Stick to Your Plan 37
    Chapter 10: Strategic Planning 39
    Chapter 11: Setting Goals 45
SECTION IV: Deepen Your Diligence 49
    Chapter 12: Following Up 51
    Chapter 13: Getting Things Done 55
    Chapter 14: Preparing and Practicing 59
    Chapter 15: Mastering Time 63
    Chapter 16: Delegating 69
    Chapter 17: Purging 73
    Chapter 18: Developing Self-Discipline 77
    Chapter 19: Saving and Investing 81

SECTION V: Sharpen Your Tools 87
    Chapter 20: Using Email Effectively 89
    Chapter 21: Tracking Progress 97
    Chapter 22: Using Checklists 101
    Chapter 23: Filing 105
    Chapter 24: Running Meetings 107
    Chapter 25 Using Good Systems 111
SECTION VI: Strengthen Your Relationships 115
    Chapter 26: Getting and Giving Feedback 117
    Chapter 27: Showing Appreciation 123
    Chapter 28: Communicating 129
    Chapter 29: Clarifying Expectations 137
    Chapter 30: Networking 141
    Chapter 31: Conducting Performance Evaluations 145
    Chapter 32: Managing Up 149
SECTION VII: Learn Your Whole Life Long 153
    Chapter 33: Reading 155
    Chapter 34: Learning 159
    Chapter 35: Having Mentors 163
    Chapter 36: Using Coaching 167
CONCLUSION 171
EXPERTS CITED 173
ABOUT THE AUTHOR 177

ACKNOWLEDGMENTS

First, I want to thank my wonderful family for supporting me through this endeavor, especially my loving wife of 43 years, Elizabeth, my two sons, Alan and Jeff, daughter-in-law Karen, and four energetic grandsons, Troup, Will, Alexander, and Andras.

Then I want to mention the wise and talented leaders in the nonprofit sector, especially my fellow CEO's, with whom I worked for over 25 years. I learned from them and adopted many of their ideas and suggestions.

Next would be the thoughtful and godly people with whom I rub shoulders in my ministry work, mainly through Young Life where I have been a volunteer coach and consultant for over 10 years.

I am grateful to my superb editor and consultant, Susan Ward for her significant contribution to this book. In addition to terrific editing and helping to organize the structure and layout, she helped mightily in getting the book published.

Lastly, I want to thank Meghan Ward for designing the book's cover and graphic content.

PREFACE

Years ago, when I set up my consulting business web site, a colleague suggested that I post a simple wisdom tip each month. As the years went by and the collection of wisdom snippets grew, I began to think that gathering and fleshing out some of these ideas into short chapters might be helpful to others. Hence, this book. My goal in writing this little primer was to create a collection of practical advice for being successful in life.

Regardless of our age or stage, we all face the same challenges of living in a fast-paced and distracted culture. We are inundated with good ideas. But most are never implemented. Why not? Because we get distracted or are caught up in the tyranny of the urgent. Or because the good ideas come in a form that doesn't facilitate getting from head to habit.

To get from tips to transformation, guidance must come in a format that is both easily digestible and implementable. Learning and applying a few of the ideas contained in this book could have a profound effect on your life. But few people have either the time or the inclination to read whole books on practical subjects like planning, goal setting, organization, time management, email processing, delegating, etc. Most would prefer to read a short chapter and get a couple of strategies they could begin to implement right away.

Instead of reading this book straight through (although I would recommend that as well), many may prefer to consult the Table of Contents and go to the chapter that addresses their most pressing need. In that way, this little book could serve as a continuing resource for people who seek to adopt new life management habits.

As I wrote this book, I had several groups of people in mind.

First, it is for folks starting out in adult life and/or their careers (oh, how I wish I had something like this when I first began working!) who could benefit from practical tips to start off on the right foot to negotiate life well.

Second, it is for those who are in the middle of their lives/careers who want to "up their game" in managing life's challenges.

Third, it is for people in ministry and faith-based organizations. Such people tend to be highly relational and called to minister to others. Often, however, those who are strong relationally need help in areas such as organization, discipline, systems, etc.

Fourth, it is for a much broader audience that includes people in all stages of life: students, parents raising children, grown kids returning to the nest, people reentering the work after several years, retirees, etc.

I am indebted to many people for the ideas compiled in this primer. I learned them from years of reading a wide variety of experts. These include David Allen, Stephen Covey, Brian Tracy, and so on. I have implemented many of their concepts in unique ways and explain that in various chapters. When I can remember the source, I provide a reference. In some cases, I cannot identify a source. Please rest assured, however, that I do not want to take credit for another's thinking. I am grateful for having many wise teachers.

My hope and prayer is that within these pages, you will find many valuable suggestions that you can integrate into your life to enrich your relationships, your work, and your day-to-day existence in ways that will make them more satisfying, more enjoyable, and more lovely.

SECTION I
Elevate Your Habits

CHAPTER 1

Become a Champion at Developing Excellent Habits

"People do not decide their futures, they decide their habits and their habits decide their futures."

F.M. Alexander

To be successful in your life and your work, develop excellent habits. In fact, this is probably the single most important thing you can do. Hear Aristotle: *"We are what we repeatedly do. Excellence, then, is not an act but a habit."* This notion is simple to grasp yet can be quite difficult to apply. It is not surprising that many people don't make greater efforts to build strong habits into their lives. We often experience challenges going from ideas to practice.

Many books have been written about habits but one, <u>The Power of Focus,</u> by Canfield, Hansen, and Hewitt, contains outstanding advice. I have summarized some of their thoughts below.

Guess what? Successful people have good habits. And unsuccessful people usually do not. In fact, some estimate that over 90% of our success in life depends on our habits. A habit is nothing more than a behavior that you repeat, over and over again. The often-quoted theory that it takes twenty-one days to develop a new habit has been largely debunked. It turns out to depend on the nature of the new behavior. Some habits take much longer to develop and there are probably a few that take less time.

When giving presentations, I often share the following riddle (the author is anonymous) with the audience one paragraph at a time and ask how many can guess the answer.

WHO AM I?

> I am your constant companion. I am your greatest helper or heaviest burden. I am completely at your command. Half the things you do you might as well turn over to me, and I will be able to do them quickly and correctly.

> I am easily managed – you must merely be firm with me. Show me exactly how you want something done and, after a few lessons, I will do it automatically. I am the servant of all great people and, alas, of all failures as well. Those who are great, I have made great. Those who are failures, I have made failures

> I am not a machine though I work with all the precision of a machine plus the intelligence of a human being. Take me, train me, be firm with me, and I will place the world at your feet. Be easy with me and I will destroy you.

WHO AM I?
I AM... HABIT!

Very few people figure it out even after all three paragraphs are shown. Here is the challenge: good habits are hard to make and easy to keep. But bad habits are easy to make and hard to break. In fact, Charles Duhigg wrote a terrific book, <u>The Power of Habit,</u> that contains some of the science behind habits. He contends that habits consist of three parts: the *cue* (which triggers the habit or the automatic behavior), the *routine* (which is the actual behavior), and the *reward* (something the person values or enjoys). Of course, there is a lot more to it, but that is the essence of Duhigg's explanation of how to establish good habits and defeat bad habits.

In the same vein, in <u>The Way We're Working Isn't Working</u>, Tony Schwartz and Jim Loehr contend that that fully 95% of our behavior occurs out of habit, either unconsciously or in reaction to external cues. They observe, *"Every great performer we've encountered – musicians, heart surgeons, dancers, FBI agents, athletes, and leaders – intuitively understands the power of making key behaviors automatic."*

The good news is that you can reprogram yourself any time you choose. Bad habits can be broken. While it may take significant effort, it's worth it.

Now for the bad news – the results of our habits usually don't show up until much later. If they showed up right away, one would have an immediate incentive to change them. For example, a person who smokes doesn't experience the destructive effect that smoking has on the body until years later when faced with cancer or heart problems. Thus, the need to be both wise and intentional about the habits we establish.

I encourage you to think about habits in two ways: those you would like to establish and those you already have that are not serving you well. Your list of helpful habits will likely be different from mine. Here are several habits that are long-time routines in my life:

- Spend time with the Lord each morning.
- Use the first hour of the workday well.
- Set monthly, weekly, and daily goals.
- Work from a daily To-Do list.
- Capture everything I must do on lists (and not in my head).
- Exercise regularly.
- Ensure excellent follow-up.

And here are some unhelpful habits that I have worked hard to break:

- Not listening well.

- Not leaving for appointments in enough time (so I either must rush to get there or arrive late).
- Not spending enough time with my family.
- Procrastinating on some things.

In his fascinating book, The Productivity Project, Chris Bailey describes compound interest and how it accumulates as one of his favorite things. He notes, "*The exact same thing is true with incremental changes you make with your habits. Not many people write books on the power of making tiny, incremental changes to the way you live and work, probably because the idea isn't all that sexy. But it works better than anything else.*" He is right on target.

Work on one habit at a time. Not three habits or even two but one habit. Just one! Work on it and, once you are certain you have mastered it, tackle a second one.

Here is a helpful tip: the best way to break a bad habit is to substitute a good habit for it. For example, to break my bad habit of waiting until the last minute to leave for an appointment, I set in advance a time that I must be in my car and pulling out of the driveway. Additionally, to encourage myself in this, I keep track of how many "on time" departures I achieve per month versus how many failures. That makes it more fun for me and it is working.

Finally, here are three quotes that I have found helpful:

"*You've got to be before you can do; you've got to do before you can have.*"

Zig Ziglar

"*Habits are like financial capital – forming one today is an investment that will automatically give out returns for years to come.*"

William James

"*The easier you are on yourself when no one is around, the harder life is going to be on you.*"

Jim Rohn

The truth is that, by systematically changing one behavior at a time, you can significantly improve your life. Wow! If I could improve my life by this approach, count me in! How about you?

Getting Started

1) Identify one unproductive habit and decide what productive habit you will replace it with. Make a simple written plan to implement that wise decision.
2) Identify one new positive habit and make a simple written plan to achieve it. Then, go to work and implement your plan.
3) To increase your rate of success, consider asking one trusted and disciplined friend or colleague to review your plan and suggest changes to make success more likely.

Chapter 2

Become a Champion at Using the Mini Habit Approach

"Be the person with embarrassing goals and impressive results instead of one of the many people with impressive goals and embarrassing results."

Stephen Guise

In his great little book entitled <u>Mini Habits</u>, Stephen Guise argues that because good habits are hard to form (true!), most of us never establish them. One effective way to overcome this barrier is to begin a *"mini habit,"* which Guise calls *"stupidly small."* Such habits are so small that you don't need much willpower or motivation to begin and stick to them. This is helpful because both willpower and motivation can be significant stumbling blocks for most of us in establishing positive habits.

One mini habit Guise cites, for example, is to do one pushup a day. How much effort does that take? Not much. If you are in bed at night and remember it, all that is required is to hop out of bed and do one. Easy! The rule is that you <u>must</u> do one, but you can <u>never</u> raise the bar. If you raised your pushup goal to five or ten, you might not be so quick to jump out of bed and keep this habit going. Thus, you never raise the bar above one. The other rule is that you do not have to stop there. While you are on the floor doing one pushup, how easy it is to do two or three…or ten?

I began this mini habit on June 8, 2015. My wife and I were in Chicago for a long weekend. When I finished reading Guise's book, I put it down, dropped to the floor and did about three pushups right there in our hotel room. I am sorry to say that I could not do a lot more than that. It is now more than five years later and – ready for this? – I have not missed a day yet! I am so committed to this "mini habit" that when I travel, I put "*Do Pushups!*" signs in my suitcase so I do not forget and miss a day.

On most days I usually do thirty or forty pushups, but all I must do is one. No pressure. The result? In the last five years, I have likely done more than 50,000 pushups. Am I healthier for it? You bet! Recently my wife remarked on how much stronger and robust my upper body looks. It is amazing what one mini habit can do to improve one's life. Adding another mini habit will improve things even more.

Getting Started

Spend a few thoughtful minutes identifying one new habit you would like to adopt. Then, think about what small step (i.e., mini habit) that would not take much willpower or motivation you could incorporate to move you in that direction.

For example, suppose you want to learn a foreign language. You might commit to spending at least three minutes every day learning Spanish. That sure will not take much willpower or motivation. Just set your timer for three minutes (or four or five) and review a list of words, turn on Rosetta Stone, engage Duolingo (a great app!), etc. On many days, when the timer rings, you will want to keep going.

Chapter 3

Become a Champion at Implementing

"Knowing is not enough, we must apply. Willing or not, we must do."

Goethe

I was on a conference call a few years ago when someone said, *"Implementation is everything."* I have known that and believed it for years but the way my colleague said it in such a simple, matter-of-fact way really hit home with me. How many people dream big dreams and make great plans but never get around to accomplishing them. It is all about implementation. This is an essential skill. If you develop a successful system to ensure superb implementation, your work and your life will improve.

Motivational speaker Brian Tracy says the mark of an effective person is what he does when he takes in new information. When such a person hears a good idea, she writes it down, processes it and acts on it. Compare that to the person who hears a good idea and does nothing with it.

Think about that. When I do presentations, I often tell my audiences to try to get something from the presentation. It could be one new idea, one new habit to establish, one new book to buy and read, one new resource to explore, one new technique to try. The key is to make the time worthwhile even if the lecturer is not terribly interesting or compelling. As Jim Rohn used to say, *"Try to get something from the day (to make you better) rather than just getting through the day."*

One new idea, habit, or practice – if implemented – can change your life. Effective people are action-oriented, while others are talk-oriented. Put another way, author, Stephen Covey said, "*Remember, to <u>know</u> and not to <u>do</u> is really not to know.*" Author and speaker Les Brown states, "*You don't have to be great to get started but you have to get started to be great.*"

So, how does an idea get executed? The short answer is that you must have a workable and trusted system that enables you to implement consistently and well. Find and perfect a system that works well for you.

A tactic I have found useful to enhance implementation is to identify my "*big rocks*" (the most important items to work on or complete each week) and block out time on my calendar to tackle them. I treat these the same way I would treat any other appointment. If someone suggests a meeting or activity when I have a project on my calendar, I politely decline with the explanation that I have a conflict with another appointment. Which I do – with myself!

Note: I take care to put only a few of these items on my calendar because the calendar is only for appointments or tasks that must be completed on a specific day at a specific time.

In his book, <u>The Productivity Project</u>, Chris Bailey points out that productivity has nothing to do with how much you *do* and everything to do with how much you *accomplish*. Furthermore, he contends that the best way to measure productivity is to ask yourself a simple question at the end of every day: Did I get done what I intended to? If the answer is yes, then you were productive.

Try some of these ideas and see what you think. The key for you – and for me – is that each of us must develop an approach that serves us best. The bottom line: To become more successful in whatever you do, become an implementer! Become a doer!

Getting Started

There are many ways to start becoming a better implementer. Ultimately, having a great system is the key. One way to begin is to adopt a technique Bailey uses to work deliberately and with intention every day: The Rule of Three. Decide what three things you want to accomplish by the end of the day and rank them. Write them down, start with #1 and work to implement it. If you only get #1 done today, it has been a good day. If you get two or all three done today, it will have been a fabulous day.

SECTION II
Own Your Life

Chapter 4

Become a Champion at Designing Your Ideal Life

"We can change our lives. We can do, have, and be exactly what we wish."

Tony Robbins

It is essential to become intentional about planning for the future. I am a huge advocate of planning your day, your week, your month, your year, and even longer periods. I have always had long-range goals with shorter-term goals flowing from them for the current year. I then break these down into monthly objectives in support of those goals. (See Chapter 11 on setting goals.)

Brian Tracy, in his wonderful book, Time Power, describes one approach to life planning. He declares the next five years will pass anyway, so you and I will be much better off if we design them than if we just go with the flow. He recommends that individuals (and I think this could work with couples as well) undertake a process of designing their ideal lives for a point five years in the future. Imagine what your perfect life would look like five years from now. Dream a little. Then, write up a description in several detailed paragraphs or pages. Be as specific as possible. Tracy suggests several questions to get started and I have added a few of my own:

- Where will you be?
- Who will you be with? What kind of love relationship will you have?

- What kinds of other relationships will you have and with whom?
- What will you be doing? What will your career look like?
- How much will you be earning? What will your net worth be?
- What will your health be like? How will you be maintaining/improving it?
- What will your spiritual life be like?
- What interests and hobbies will you be pursuing?
- How will you be growing and improving?

Here are some additional questions with an even longer horizon:
- If you could write your autobiography, what would it say?
- What do you imagine (hope) that people would say about you at your funeral – a close friend, a professional colleague, a close family member, and your clergyman?
- If you could write your own eulogy, to be read by your friends and relatives at your funeral, what would it say?
- What would you dare to dream if you knew you could not fail?
- What do you really love to do, at home and at work?

You get the idea. This is a worthwhile exercise. If you are married, share this with your spouse. In fact, he or she may want to join you in this exercise and then you can compare to see whether your dreams are similar. If not, that calls for an important discussion.

Once you have written this plan down, thought about it, and polished it, you must develop goals and objectives to accomplish it. And finally, you just commit to implementing them. For example, if you state in your plan that you want to have several close personal lifetime friends, what do you need to start doing today to bring that about? Or, if you want to weigh a trim, athletic 180 pounds, have smoke-free lungs, and be in tip-top physical shape, what must you begin doing today to make that happen? Just like with investing money, even small actions, compounded over time can add up to a wonderful life.

Getting Started

Set aside an hour in a quiet place where you will not be disturbed. Rough out what your ideal life would look like in five years and write it down or type it up. Use the questions above to catalyze your thinking or come up with your own. Then set it aside for a day or two. Return to it and see if it still makes sense. You will likely modify it somewhat and that is good. If you are married, go through this process with your spouse to ensure both of you are on the same page. Once you are satisfied with your plan, develop goals and objectives to make this ideal future a reality.

Chapter 5

Become a Champion at Taking Responsibility

"When a person denies responsibility for the movement and direction of his life, he almost automatically fails."

John Malloy

There appears to be a trend these days of people failing to take responsibility for their lives – both in their work and their personal lives. Our first reaction when something goes wrong often is to find someone to blame. We look for someone or something to point at other than us because, "it can't be me!" This is a worrisome development that affects us and those around us.

Charlie Plumb, a U. S. Navy fighter pilot, once addressed my organization. He described his experience of being a prisoner of war in a North Vietnam prison for seven years. He began his remarks by pacing up and down on the stage – a few feet in one direction and then a few feet in the other, and then observing, *"This was the size of my home for seven years."* He told us that many prisoners-of-wars survived confinement – and even torture – and then succeeded and thrived after their release. His speech was compelling. Many years later, though, what I particularly remember is one thing he said: *"It's not what's around you that matters; it's how you deal with what is around you."*

Think about the profound meaning of that statement. If we wait until everything around us is optimal, we will never succeed because there will always be impediments. That is how life is. I have made a list of all the excuses people make for why they have not done as well in life as they would like.

Reasons People Give for Not Succeeding in Life:

> Home State/City   Government
> Siblings   Company Culture
> Bad Luck   Things Cost Too Much
> Parents   Negative Relatives   Boss
> Spouse   Not Enough Time
> Coworkers
> Traffic   Heredity
> Not Enough Money   Weather
> Education   Past Experiences
> Economy
> Nosy Neighbors
> People Don't Like Me

Do any items on the list resonate with you? There are several that I employed in the past. Please do not misunderstand me. Many of the above are legitimate impediments to success. However, I believe it is time to stop focusing on these limitations and instead focus on what you can do. Ask yourself this question: Is there anyone in similar circumstances who has succeeded? The answer is, "Of course."

To me, here is the bottom line. Under God's guidance, you and I are responsible for everything we are, become and achieve. We need to fully accept responsibility, understanding that roadblocks and setbacks will surely occur, and we need to persevere. The goal is never to make excuses or blame others, or to play the victim or the loser. Brian Tracy sometimes puts it, *"if it is to be, it's up to me."*

John Malloy, author of <u>Dress for Success</u> and <u>Living for Success</u>, says, *"When a person denies responsibility for the movement and direction of his life, he almost automatically fails."* He also says that one universal characteristic of failures is their lack of energy.

Brian Tracy introduces an interesting concept when he says, *"Between stimulus and response, there is a space. In that space lies our freedom and power to choose our response. In those choices lie our growth and our happiness."* This is how we are different from animals. With them, there is no space between stimulus and response. That is also true of some humans who are used to responding immediately – and often inappropriately – without some careful thought.

The bottom line, then, is that we should all strive for and live in a way that we take responsibility for our lives and the challenges we face. Having this attitude can make all the difference.

Getting Started

First, I might suggest that you resolve for today to stop 1) making excuses and 2) blaming anyone else for unfavorable things that happen in your life. Then resolve the same thing tomorrow and stick to it, then the next day and so on until it becomes a habit. Second, you could decide what you can do to keep moving forward despite the obstacles. Third, make a simple action plan and implement it. The key is to act!

Chapter 6

Become a Champion at Living Near Your Ideal Busyness Level

"Never confuse activity with productivity."

Rick Warren

What is your ideal busyness level? When working one-on-one with clients, one of my favorite coaching questions is: *"If 100 is your ideal busyness level, where are you now?"* Some of us like to be busier than others, so the ideal is different for each of us. The key part of the question is where the person is compared to her ideal. If a person is operating at 80 or 85, he is probably bored. Between 95 and 105 is perfect. If someone is at 120, she is getting near the edge and at 140, the person is probably experiencing considerable stress and disfunction.

This question about busyness is an effective and simple way to determine what an individual is experiencing in his life. The principle underlying the question is that we are happiest and most productive when we operate close to our ideal busyness level. It is not healthy to function substantially under it for too long because it creates a temptation to slack off, develop some less than helpful habits and/or even getting involved in some unhealthy activities. Likewise, it is quite unhealthy – both physically and mentally – to function significantly above it. Being too busy often leads to frustration, burnout, and an unhealthy attitude. Crunch periods are one thing. Most of us experience them and handle them quite well – for a limited time. Tax accountants experience a crunch in March and April of each year. College students put in long hours during finals. A litigation attorney will do the same during trials.

The problem arises when we are expected to consistently operate and perform at a busyness level much higher than we can reasonably handle. We only have twenty-four hours in each day, so something must go: we sacrifice sleep, exercise, time with our families, recreation, worship, etc. This unhealthy state – if it lasts for too long – usually results in a lower job performance and a reduction in the quality of life.

Once we determine realistically where we are, we can identify some strategies to help move closer to our ideal. This strategizing is best done with a trusted friend, coach, or counselor who can help us be honest with ourselves and about our circumstances. One's family should be involved, especially if major life changes are considered. This is an essential and healthy undertaking. It may take some time but as long as one sees progress moving in the right direction, there is hope. The best solution may involve a thoughtful reordering of one's life. Extreme situations may require a job change.

Getting Started

Determine your current busyness level compared to your ideal. Ask yourself honestly where you are today. Do this on several different days so you get a fair reading. It may help to ask someone close to you for his perspective. Once you have a good sense of where you are, assess the situation and identify some steps to take that will move you closer to your ideal. Implement one, then another until you reach that ideal level of busyness.

Chapter 7

Become a Champion at Being Positive, Optimistic, and Happy

"Optimism is a tremendously powerful predictor of work performance."

Shawn Achor

A large body of research points to the advantages enjoyed by those who are positive, optimistic, and happy. Many of us tend to "see the glass half empty" rather than "see the glass half full." We often expect the worst to happen and that expectation increases the likelihood that it will.

Psychologist Martin Seligman is considered the father of the positive psychology movement. He points to research showing that optimistic people are happier, healthier, and more successful than those with a negative perspective on life. The biblical wisdom book of Proverbs affirms this (e.g., *"A cheerful heart is good medicine"* – Proverbs 17:22). People respond far better to those who are cheerful and optimistic than to those who are gloomy and pessimistic.

While many people assume optimism vs. pessimism is an immutable personality trait, Seligman's research (among others) demonstrates that optimism can be learned. The underlying dynamics are habits of thinking and our ways of interpreting events can be changed. In fact, this single change in outlook, if one will adopt it, will pay dividends in many ways.

Pastor Charles Swindoll gives us a great reminder that life is full of opportunities:

"The longer I live, the more I realize the impact of attitude on life. Attitude, to me, is more important than education, than money, than circumstances, than failures, than successes, than what other people think or say or do. It is more important than appearance, giftedness, or skill. It will make or break a company . . . a church . . . a home. The remarkable thing is we have a choice every day regarding the attitude we will embrace for the day. We cannot change our past . . . we cannot change the fact people will act in a certain way. We cannot change the inevitable. The only thing we can do is play on the one string we have, and that is our attitude. I am convinced that life is 10% what happens to me and 90% how I react to it. And so it is with you. We are in charge of our attitudes."

In his fascinating little book, <u>The Happiness Advantage,</u> Shawn Achor observes that most of us follow a formula that has been taught to us overtly or more subtly by our schools, our employers, our parents, and society: if you work hard, you will become successful and then you will be happy. Achor says this pattern of belief explains what most often motivates us in life. He asserts that this formula is broken.

Achor contends that the relationship between happiness and success works the other way around. Science now shows that happiness is the forerunner of success, not merely the result. Happiness and optimism fuel performance and achievement. He calls this "the happiness advantage." Achor contends that when the brain is happier, it performs significantly better than when it is neutral or stressed. In fact, one study showed that happier people are 31% more productive.

Achor (and others) suggest writing down three good things that happen to you each day. They can include simple, small pleasures such as a good night's sleep, a great lunch with a friend, a lovely sunny day, the completion of a difficult project, etc. Anchor maintains that writing down three good things that happened to you that day forces your brain to scan the last 24 hours for potential positives. In just five minutes a day, this practice trains the brain to become more skilled at noticing and focusing on possibilities for personal and professional growth and seizing opportunities to act on them.

I am blessed by being naturally positive and optimistic. But I can always learn more, so I began this habit of writing down three good things some years ago. I have never had to look too hard to find rays of sunshine even in otherwise challenging days. I have observed how simply writing down three little positives every day can improve my mood and outlook.

Jim Rohn offers a challenge: If you wish to be happy, study happiness. Happiness is not an accident; it is a choice. If you want happiness, you must take steps to design it into your life.

Getting Started

1) Begin by adopting Shawn Achor's suggestion to write down three good things that happen to you each day. Just doing that will improve your spirits and happiness.
2) Another option is to identify one negative tendency or habit you have and resolve to change it. For example, if you tend to assume a negative narrative about circumstances, you can adopt the habit of switching that negative interpretation for a positive one. If a friend or colleague does not return your phone call in a timely manner, you could assume that he does not like or respect you. Or you could practice shifting to a more positive (and likely) explanation, such as the person was juggling many projects at work or missed the voice mail. If you tend to assume the worst about others, you can shift that interpretation to one of charitable judgment about them. For example, if a friend arrives late for your lunch appointment, rather than labeling her as selfish, you could consider the range of other possibilities (e.g., traffic, difficulty finding parking, a last-minute project at work) that offer a more charitable explanation for her tardiness.

Chapter 8

Become a Champion at Employing Positive Self Talk

"Consistent positive self-talk is unquestionably one of the greatest gifts to one's subconscious mind."

Edmond Mbiaka

Author Brian Tracy believes our self-talk largely determines our success in life. In fact, he says that 95% of our emotions are determined by how we talk to ourselves. Think about all the things you say to yourself throughout an average day. Are they positive or negative? Do you find your self-talk consisting of statements such as:
- How stupid! What is wrong with you?
- I cannot seem to do anything right.
- Oh, boy. I must be a real loser.
- I will probably blow this sale too.
- That person got really upset. It must be my fault.
- I am a terrible person.

Or are there more statements like these:
- Things generally work out well for me.
- I messed up this particular task, but that does not define how I generally do things.
- I learned from this mistake and will do better next time.
- While I lost the last sale, I am confident that I will make others; I usually do.
- That person got really upset. She must be having a bad day.

- A year from now, how much will this really matter?
- This too shall pass.

Negative self-talk involves conflating events and character/skills. Engaging in habitually putting yourself down, however unconsciously, has significant negative effects on your well-being and your performance. Over time, these negative descriptions etch a groove in one's head and a person begins to believe them. Even worse, they become self-fulfilling prophecies. People begin to act based on how they see themselves.

In contrast, positive self-talk separates what happened (what we did or was done to us) from one's value (our character and abilities). Our explanatory style (what we tell ourselves about an experience) determines how we react to a situation. Such talk is much healthier and usually allows a bad experience to dissipate rather than bog us down. For most of us, talking to ourselves positively does not come naturally.

As with all skills, we must train ourselves to think and talk to ourselves this way. Over time, it can make a significant difference in our happiness, our performance, and our lives. The goal is to eliminate negative self-talk and replace it with positive self-talk. How does one do this?

The first step is to cultivate the ability to notice what your self-talk is like. When you pay attention, you will begin to see patterns. Then, when you notice a negative explanation or phrase frequently popping into your head, develop a positive alternative. You must cultivate the ability to speak to yourself rather than listen to yourself. The key is to build a new habit in one area and then, once locked in, expand it to gradually cover all self-talk. This will take time and effort, but you will be glad you did.

Getting Started

1) Choose one of the negative phrases from the first list above and think about how you would replace it with a positive

alternative. Or notice a phrase you often say to yourself and develop a new one instead. Try to monitor yourself. It is sometimes helpful to ask a friend or family member to point out to you what they hear you saying. We often are not even aware of our negative self-talk.

2) Practice the positive self-talk as needed. Over time it will become a new habit. Then focus on the next phrase. Developing a habit of affirming self-talk will make real difference in your outlook.

Chapter 9

Become a Champion at Following the 80-20 Rule

"80% of the results come from 20% of the causes. A few things are important; most things are not."

Richard Koch

A highly effective way to prioritize things in your life is to implement the Pareto principle (also known as the 80-20 rule). It states that, for many things, roughly 80 percent of the effects arise from 20 percent of the causes.

Italian economist Vilfredo Pareto observed that about 20 percent of the peapods in his garden produced 80 percent of the peas. He developed the concept to describe the distribution of wealth in Italy: he showed that approximately 80 percent of the wealth in Italy was owned by 20 percent of the population.

In the 1940s, management consultant Joseph Juran adapted Pareto's principle to manufacturing quality control. He demonstrated that by focusing on 20 percent of the processes, defects could be substantially reduced, resulting in a significant improvement in quality.

In recent decades, this 80/20 rule has become popularized as a management principle and many have written about it. Examples include:
- In sales, 80 percent of the profits come from 20 percent of the sales.
- In many groups, 20 percent of the people do 80 percent of the work.

- 80 percent of our success and accomplishments comes from 20 percent of our activities.

Think about this in your life and see if it isn't true. The key is to focus your attention and effort on these few (roughly 20 percent) things that will yield the biggest payoff. As Jim Rohn said, *"Don't spend major time on minor things – spend major time on major things."*

What are the 20 percent of things in your life and/or work that matter most? The first step is to be clear about what they are. This will likely take some careful attention, thought and prayer. Ask yourself, *"What things, if done extremely well, would result in the greatest positive impact in my life and work?"* Invariably, a handful of things will come to mind. These are the 20 percent on which you should focus.

Develop a plan to make these things a priority in your life. Ultimately, these priority areas should receive more of your attention, time, effort, and resources. Elevating these things in your life will require deemphasizing others. If everything is a priority, then nothing is a priority. Over time, you will see payoff in focusing on improving the 20 percent. Your choices will better align with your heartfelt values.

Getting Started

Find a quiet place alone where you can think. Set aside at least thirty minutes and have a pad of paper with you. Identify the most important things in your life and write them down. Then go back and refine them. Some items may drop off your list and you may think of others to add. Continue to refine them until you feel confident that you have your 20 percent. Then spend some time strategizing how you can focus on these areas.

SECTION III
Stick to Your Plan

Chapter 10

Become a Champion at Strategic Planning

"A plan is not putting you in a box and forcing you to stay there. A plan is a guide to keep you on course, efficient, and safe."

Amber Hurdle

There are dozens of ways to do strategic planning. The key is finding a process that works for you and/or your organization and that creates an implementable plan to lead the organization forward.

I was introduced to strategic planning around 1991. I had been in my CEO position for five or six years and was increasingly frustrated by not having a plan to guide our association. It came to light one year during my annual evaluation. Having nothing to measure my performance against (i.e., a strategic plan), my board members wandered all over the place. One of them thought I was doing a good job but wished I had addressed one goal. Another board member asked whether they had ever directed me to accomplish that goal. The first board member acknowledged the board had not but thought perhaps I should have done it anyway. A third board member then expressed that he did not care about that goal but had another as a priority. And on it went. I decided then and there that we needed clear direction for where the organization wanted to go.

I found Jack Schlegel, a talented strategic planning professional to assist us. He spent two days with a committee of board leaders, a cross section of association members, and senior staff. With his help, we produced an excellent strategic plan. Jack urged us to update or refresh the plan annually and we did, bringing him back every year at our board retreat to lead us in the update. The plan developed and changed each year for some 20 years and truly kept us on track. The plan also gave my board a solid basis to assess my performance, one based on objective (and not only subjective) measurements.

This experience gave me a deep appreciation for strategic planning. As a result, I began helping various groups within my church with planning. One day, the executive director of a local free clinic called and asked me to help that organization do strategic planning. That clinic became my first client, and I began a consulting firm focused on strategic planning. Over the years, I have led more than fifty groups in strategic planning, using the same process and philosophical framework that Jack Schlegel taught me. The results have been uniformly positive.

Many successful approaches to strategic planning exist. What follows is just one example.

I. Elements of Effective Strategic Plans

Strategic planning consultants define terms and nomenclature differently. What follows is my approach to identifying the elements of an effective strategic planning.

1) Mission/Purpose Statement: Defines clear focus and direction for the organization. The statement answers some or all the questions: Who are we? Whom do we represent/serve? What are we trying to accomplish? What business are we in?

2) Vision Statement: Clear, compelling statement of what the organization aspires to be in three years. Ideally, what will it look like? The vision should be so clear and powerful that people will feel strong desire to work to achieve it.

3) Goals: Major focuses of the organization that will support the vision and set the overall direction for the next three years. The ideal number is three to six major goals.

4) Objectives: *What* is to be achieved under each goal during the next three years. Objectives must be specific, measurable, and

written as outcomes. Strive to write two to six *SMART* objectives for each goal (see below).
SMART stands for:
   S pecific
   M easurable
   A chievable
   R ealistic
   T ime-based.

5) Action Steps: *How* each objective is to be achieved. Action steps must be specific and include due dates and names of individuals and/or groups who are responsible for achieving them. Writing them down at the planning stage forces the group members to think through the tasks up front. Accomplishing these action steps will ensure the objectives are successfully met. Note: action steps are not determined during the strategic planning day-long session but are determined later by staff who are going to accomplish them.

II. Preliminary Steps

1) Get stakeholder buy-in and commitment to the importance of strategic planning. Involve a wide variety of people, including board members, key leadership, staff, major donors, key volunteers, members/constituents, etc. The point is to seek feedback from a larger, rather than narrower group of people.

2) Engage a professional strategic planner. It is difficult for a member of an organization – especially the CEO or other leader – to direct a group in planning without impeding the free flow of ideas. Furthermore, it is nearly impossible to facilitate a process while trying to participate in the discussions. Thus, getting an outsider, preferably a professional planner, is essential.

3) Determine the planning group. Opinions vary but my preference is to have a planning group of ten to fifteen members. This size is large enough to include a good cross section of people with different perspectives, experience, and way of thinking, but not so large that it gets bogged down.

4) Survey your constituency. This is a critical step, particularly because everyone cannot be on the planning group or committee. I recommend that organizations survey all their key stakeholders. The survey can contain a mix of rating scales and narrative comment. For the latter, it is important to include all the responses in the report, so the planning group has a deep understanding of the survey feedback. The responses will be compiled (usually by a trusted staff member) in an unattributed manner for each survey question. A week before the planning session, the planning group will receive a document containing all the input at a granular level but without anyone knowing who said what.

5) Schedule a day-long planning session. It typically takes most of a day for an organization to develop a good first draft of a strategic plan.

III. Process of Developing Strategic Plan

The mission, vision, goals, and objectives are the "whats." The leadership group/planning committee determines them. Action steps, on the other hand, are the "hows." Generally speaking, operational staff (those who have the responsibility to accomplish the action steps) determine this level of the strategic plan.

After the planning session concludes, I recommend that the facilitator write up the first draft of the committee's work and distribute it to the committee for comments and edits. When I facilitate strategic planning processes, I do not change a single word of the plan as drafted in the planning session but put it in a clear and understandable format.

Once we gather the feedback from the committee, I recommend that a smaller group (usually the chairman of the organization, the CEO, several other members of the planning committee, and an additional staff person) meet to "scrub the plan." I walk them through the plan section by section, and we look critically at all the words and thoughts, what they mean and if they are clear and understandable to others. I also push the CEO to come to this meeting prepared to suggest that we alter some of the tentative due dates that were set at the planning session. In my experience, groups tend to be too ambitious and 75-80 percent of the due dates are initially set during the first year of a three-year plan.

Once this is completed, I produce a second draft for the scrub group to review and once they approve it, I or the CEO distributes it to the broader planning group for its review. Once the entire committee is comfortable with the plan, it is given to appropriate staff to develop the action steps required to implement the plan. This encourages them to do their thinking up front. If the people who will be doing the work to accomplish the plan take the time to think through – ahead of time – how they will go about implementing the objectives in the plan and write these steps out, implementation will be significantly easier. Furthermore, this step is an important check on the timeframes established in the plan. If staff identify steps that cannot be accomplished by the initial dates, they can suggest to the planning scrub group that the dates by altered before the plan is finalized.

Once the action steps are completed, the entire plan is assembled and presented to the board or governing body for its final review and approval. This usually takes less than an hour. Once that body adopts the strategic plan, we are finished, and implementation begins.

IV. Process of Implementing and Tracking Strategic Plan

I recommend that organizations carefully track progress compared to the plan and that the governing body receive a status report at least quarterly. The best way to do this is for the CEO or top staff person to use color-coding to indicate progress. Green means the objective or action step has been completed, blue means the item is in progress and yellow means the item is delayed and/or has not been completed. Using this approach enables the governing body to review the plan and ascertain the status quickly and use meeting time to focus on the parts of the plan not completed versus going through every item.

I used this process in my nonprofit organization and my board loved it. It gave us a clear sense of direction. The board held me accountable and I held my staff accountable for the progress we made (or did not make). It was a remarkably effective tool.

Getting Started

Look for an opportunity to take an organization (or a department or unit) through this type of strategic planning process. Discuss your idea with the leadership of that entity to get its blessing. Then identify several planning professionals and gain a clear understanding of each of their approaches. It may help to evaluate how consistent their approach is with the above steps. Regardless of the process, your goal is to end up with is a clear, measurable, and implementable plan.

Chapter 11

Become a Champion at Setting Goals

"Knowing is not enough, we must apply. Willing or not, we must do."

Goethe

Author Brian Tracy asserts that the ability to set goals and make plans is a master skill of life. Indeed! Having a systematic goal setting process exponentially increases the likelihood of success. There have probably been over 1,000 studies that all show the same thing: those who set goals do far, far better than those who do not. In fact, one survey showed that 80 percent of unhappy people responding had no goals. If goal setting is this powerful, why don't more people do it? I would cite the following reasons:

They do not know how to do it. They have never been taught how to set goals and objectives.

Thinking about this is hard mental work and many people shy away from that kind of work. They will work hard all day on something tangible but thinking about the future is different.

They are afraid to commit to goals and then not achieve them.

In his book, <u>The Three Signs of a Miserable Job</u>, Patrick Lencioni says, *"Employees who can measure their own progress or contribution are going to develop a greater sense of personal responsibility and satisfaction."* Individual goal setting enables this.

When I lead strategic planning sessions, I often tell groups that people and organizations, in my opinion, must only do three things to be successful:

1) Decide what you want. It is amazing how many people and organizations never intentionally decide. They do some good things, but they never really accomplish all they could. The weeks turn into months, the months turn into years, the years turn into decades and eventually it is too late.

2) Make a plan. Plans only count if they are in writing. Plans in one's head are daydreams. Committing things to writing forces clarity. The plan must be clear, measurable, and implementable.

3) Implement the plan. I have seen many organizations devote time to developing a good plan and then never implement it. It goes on the shelf and is never looked at again. Implementation is critical. (See Chapter 3 for implementation strategies.)

If you, or your company, non-profit, church, or family, takes this seriously and follows these three steps, success is sure to follow.

Chapter 10 describes how to go through a process of strategic planning that produces a series of implemental goals and objectives. Suppose, however, that you would like to begin more simply. Here is a simple yet effective approach.

1) Decide on the period of time for which you want to set some objectives (e.g., month, quarter, six months, year). If you are new to this, it will be easier to begin with a shorter period of time. For the purposes of this example, I will use a quarter.

2) Decide what you would like to accomplish during that period of time. Ask yourself or your boss, *"What would success for me look like in the next 90 days?"* At the end of the quarter, what will you be celebrating and feeling good about?

3) Brainstorm what things you might want to take on during this next quarter. Jot down ideas on an empty pad as your mind runs. Do not worry about specifics; just capture the ideas.

4) Vet the ideas and decide which ones pass muster. Begin with fewer rather than more. Remember, all the other work for which you are responsible will still be there.

5) Capture these goals as outcomes you desire. Write all objectives beginning with an action verb and as appropriate, include due dates.

Here are a few examples, related to one's personal life:
- Begin defined exercise program and track progress by (beginning date).
- Read at least one high quality non-fiction book by (date).
- Earn at least six credits toward BA degree by (date).
- Have monthly date with spouse and track progress starting (beginning date).
- Complete one-half of Level 1 Rosetta Stone Italian by (date).
- Achieve healthy weight of 180 (now 195) by (date).
- Visit brother in Maine by (date).
- Reduce credit card debt to zero (now $4,445) by (date).

Notice how all of these are outcome-based. In other words, you will know whether you have achieved them. They can all be measured.

Setting and achieving challenging objectives is one way people build self-esteem. Today's so-called "experts" who claim children can be "given" self-esteem are misguided. Give everyone a medal, no matter his or her performance. Do not keep score in games so everyone can be a winner. This sounds good, but it is not. And kids can figure it out. They keep score on their own. They know whether they are good at something or not. And you will know if you make a plan with measurable results and achieve them.

One final thought. Keith Cameron Smith, author of <u>The 10 Distinctions Between Millionaires and the Middle Class</u>, says that when one has long term goals, that person will find it easier to develop perseverance. What a great trait to develop.

Getting Started

Begin by using the steps delineated above to set several objectives. Focus on just one area of your life. This process becomes easier as you do it, and it produces tangible results. Once goal setting in this one area works for you, expand it to other parts of your life.

SECTION IV

Deepen Your Diligence

Chapter 12

Become a Champion at Following Up

"Diligent follow-up and follow-through will set you apart from the crowd and communicate excellence."

John C. Maxwell

I continue to be astonished that so many people tell you they will do something (send you something, follow up on something, etc.) but do not write it down. Predictably, they often forget and do not follow up. These omissions cause little chinks in their reputations as reliable and responsible individuals.

To become successful at most things, it is essential that one become excellent at follow up. When you commit to doing a project by a certain date, do it. If you say you will send someone a document or an article, send it. When you promise to get back to someone, keep that promise. While a failure to do these things may seem like a challenge of organization or time management, keeping one's word is at heart an issue of integrity.

Becoming excellent at follow up enhances one's reputation and character. It proves one is trustworthy. What a wonderful thing to be said about you: *"If you give it to Sally, she'll get it done."* Or: *"If Bob said he'd get back to you, he will."* That kind of reputation will pay huge dividends no matter what you do in life.

One of the best ways to earn the respect of colleagues and friends alike is to become excellent at *DWYSYWD*. Coined by Jim Kouzes and Barry Posner, it stands for *"Do What You Say You Will Do."* Focus on this one practice and incredible things will happen.

Resolving to become excellent at follow up is not enough. Good intentions and willpower alone will not get you there. Yet this problem is not difficult to remedy. There are two key strategies to conquering the failure to follow through. First, capture a commitment to do something in whatever way works best for you *at the time you make it*. Do not make the mistake of assuming you will remember it later! Some people find it helpful to type a reminder on a to-do list app on their phone, others text or email themselves a message, some enter an appointment into their calendars, while others jot it on a small notepad or even a napkin if in a restaurant. Second, transfer that commitment from where you captured it into a system where all your commitments are stored, reviewed regularly, and acted upon. This may be a digital or hand-written to-do list, a calendar, or some other method that works for you.

Notice that I said transfer it into *your system*. To do this, you must have a system or an approach to managing all your commitments. It must be a system that works for you. The best designed system will utterly fail if it does not fit your way of doing things. In Chapter 13, I discuss a system devised by David Allen and described his best-selling classic Getting Things Done. I have adopted Allen's "GTD system" and it has been a lifesaver for me. But you may find a different system that works for you.

One approach that is simple and easy to use is simply this: keep a *Master List* of everything you must or want to do. You can do this any way you like, from low-tech (write everything in a notebook or on a legal pad) to high-tech (use an app on your smart phone or laptop). This is one of my two top time management strategies.

When I was a CEO running a large, national non-profit organization, one of my best Vice Presidents always carried with her a letter-size pad of lined paper. Whenever she needed to do something (follow up on an item, capture what she had been asked or had agreed to do, etc.), she wrote it on the pad. Whenever she completed one of the tasks on her pad, she crossed it off. Once the sheet was near full, she tore it off, wrote the remaining undone items on a clean sheet and used that going forward. Every few days, the pad started looking like a real mess with new tasks scribbled on it while other items were crossed off. But this colleague never dropped a ball. She was off the charts good at follow up. And she had that simple system to thank for it. There is that word again . . . system. Find a system that works for you and you will be on your way! Parenthetically, when I stepped down from the CEO job, it was this Vice President who replaced me.

Individuals need to adopt systems to enhance follow up. The same is true for organizations. They can boost their effectiveness by developing strategies for follow up and accountability. One simple discipline can help enormously. At the end of every meeting – whether one-on-one or a group – someone ought to ask, "What are the next actions?" (David Allen's <u>Getting Things Done</u> elaborates on this). This forces the participants to agree on who is going to do what by when. Each person takes responsibility for entering the items for which he or she is responsible into his or her system and acts on them.

Getting to that level of clarity on a regular basis ensures that more will get done in a timely way and misunderstandings and confusion will be minimized. I recommend that one person be tasked to provide a summary of the agreed-upon next actions to the meeting's participants by email. Without that, the following likely scenario occurs. At the next meeting, the leader asks Joe to report on the issue that was assigned to him at last month's meeting. Joe replies, *"Was I supposed to do that? I thought Sally was doing that."* Kisha chimes in with *"No, Joe, you agreed to do that."* Sally agrees and it goes on from there. People are frustrated, no progress has been made, and a month has been lost. Documenting things in writing enhances follow up.

The bottom line: Mastering the art of following up is one practice that will enhance your reputation and make your life easier and better.

Getting Started

If you are currently using a system that you rate 8 or 9 (scale of 1-10 where 10 is high), keep using it. If not, begin your own master list. Write down everything on it that you need or want to do. Develop a habit of adding things to your list as they come up or as you think of them. Do not worry about prioritizing them. Use the list as a management tool. Review it at least once each day (and perhaps more often) and prioritize the items that you intend to accomplish that day.

Chapter 13

Become a Champion at Getting Things Done

"With a complete and current inventory of all your commitments, organized and reviewed in a systematic way, you can focus clearly and make trusted choices about what to do (and not do) at any moment."

David Allen

I always considered myself an organized person, certainly above the 50th percentile. Then I was in a bookstore in Hudson, Ohio about fifteen years ago and happened upon David Allen's best-selling book, Getting Things Done. I read it and was amazed! It made so much sense. In fact, I was so impressed that I later flew to Chicago to attend a daylong seminar with him and loved it! A year later, David Allen came to the Washington, DC area and I attended his seminar again, this time taking one of the ministers at my church and his executive assistant. I have now been to his (or his senior trainers') sessions at least ten times and I always learn something new.

To make a long story short, I have fully adopted and embraced his phenomenal approach and now teach it to others and use it in my coaching practice. I also give away copies of his classic book which now has been updated to a second edition. I recommend it highly.

I cannot do justice to Allen's book in a few paragraphs, but I will attempt to communicate the important ideas here. Allen's main thesis is that using our minds to keep track of to-do items creates untold stress on us. The goal is to clear your mind for the deeper functions like thinking creatively about how best to deal with major interests or issues.

His main strategy is to get everything you need to do or want to do out of your head and onto a series of reminders (i.e., lists). As David says so eloquently, "the mind is a terrible office." Then, you want to interact with your reminders as often as necessary to ensure you are getting things done. The lists can be as high tech or low tech as one wants. Some people use paper, others digital, and still others use a hybrid (which is the approach I use). Once your mind knows that you are using a trusted system, it no longer has to keep reminding you of all the stuff in your life (and the mind often does this at sub-optimal times like at 3 a.m. when you're trying to sleep).

The core lists Allen recommends are:
- Projects (any item that takes more than one step).
- Next Actions (single actions, including at least one for every project).
- Waiting-For (all the items you are waiting for from others – this has been invaluable to me!).
- Someday-Maybe (all those things you might want to do but are not committing to them now; you just do not want to forget them).

From there, you can have as many other lists as you think you need (calls list, errands list, agenda list for those with whom you work regularly, etc.).

One then manages from the Next Actions list (and other related lists) to ensure that those items are accomplished. For me, this works like a charm. Allen strongly recommends scheduling a weekly review. Put it on your calendar, preferably at the same time each week so that it becomes a habit. During this review, any new information (emails, paper items in an in-box, phone calls, etc.) is processed and added to the appropriate lists. Likewise, completed items are deleted from the lists. By doing this, you keep your system current.

I take this a step further and create a daily to-do list. An important key is that other than specific things I must do that day (appointments, etc.), every item must come from (or be added to) one of the Next Action lists. Why? To ensure that all items you want to accomplish are in your system. For example, suppose you wake up one morning with a new idea about something you want to do so you add it to that day's list. Then for whatever reason you do not get to it and forget to transfer it to another day. You have lost it – you might not think of it again for some time, maybe never.

A wiser course is to do one of the following: 1) add it directly to the appropriate list (which is what I do), or 2) write the idea on a piece of paper and add that into your physical in basket to be processed at your weekly review.

If your lists are paper lists and an idea arises when you do not have your lists with you (for example, you are in a restaurant), then you can write it on a napkin and put it in your pocket, record it in your smart phone, or send yourself an email. Then, when you get back to the office or home, transfer it into your system. This is why digital lists are so helpful – you always have access to them and remove the need to enter action items twice.

One of my favorite David Allen quotes is, *"Never have the same thought twice about something you have to or want to do."* You can have a hundred creative thoughts about how to manage a project or begin a new initiative, but avoid the need for repeating thoughts (e.g., *"I have to call John about the XYZ project."*) by getting those action items on your list.

Mastering this system (or any other system that works for you) enables you to become excellent at follow up (see Chapter 12) and that is one of the keys to success. As author Stephanie Winston advises in <u>Bottom Line Personal</u>, *"A disorganized life is a series of missed opportunities. Lesser concerns wind up stealing our time and energy, while people and activities we care about suffer for lack of attention."*

If you do not have and consistently use a system that works for you, I strongly recommend that you adopt one. David Allen's <u>Getting Things Done</u> has worked effectively for me.

Getting Started

To begin, I suggest you read Chapter 25, "Using Good Systems," and assess how good your current system is. Then, follow that short chapter's suggestions on finding a new system. As part of that search, I would buy and read the first 57 pages of David Allen's <u>Getting Things Done</u>. That first section describes his system quite well and will likely encourage you to read the rest of the book and consider implementing his approach.

Chapter 14

Become a Champion at Preparing and Practicing

"By failing to prepare, you are preparing to fail."

Benjamin Franklin

One key attribute for success is preparing well. Yet it is amazing how many of us do not prepare. You have probably heard the saying, *"You have to have the will to win."* This is nonsense. We all want to win. The famous Indiana basketball coach Bobby Knight had it right when he said, *"Everyone has the will to win; it's the will to prepare to win that's the key."*

I see this often in public speaking. Most people hear a terrific speaker and think, *"He's a natural"* or *"I wish I were so gifted."* Guess what? That speaker was probably not born gifted in this area. Much more likely, she developed her speaking skills through years of practice. By the time we hear her, she is probably giving her 500th talk.

I am certainly not a great public speaker, but I am good. For twenty-five years, I spoke at my association's annual meeting – to some 2,500-3000 members. At first that was a bit intimidating, but I practiced and practiced and practiced. And with each year's speech, I got better.

My church for years sponsored a Jobs Ministry to help those seeking employment. It attracted all kinds of people, from my son when he first graduated from college to the Undersecretary of the Navy. Our ministry provided spiritual and practical talks as well as small group discussions so people could learn from and encourage one another. I gave the talk on how to network to get a job. For about twenty years, I delivered the same talk (same examples, stories, etc.) three times a year. That is sixty nearly identical talks. The night before each of these talks, I practiced one more time. I had it down pat, but additional practice made me sharper and more effective.

I did the same thing before each of my board meetings when I was a CEO. I went over the agenda carefully and practiced out loud what I would say and how. I also reviewed all the agenda items in detail to make sure I could answer any questions my board members asked. This practice helped ensure effective board meetings with the desired outcomes.

The applications are endless. Those who prepare for exams do better. Those who prepare for important and often stressful conversations in their lives find that those conversations turn out better than those who give short shrift to preparation.

Public speaker and author Brian Tracy has observed that the most successful people are the most fastidious about details; unsuccessful people tend to be sloppy. This "having all your ducks in a row" is simply another way of preparing.

Preparation also requires having a good system to plan ahead so that you know what is coming your way with sufficient time to take the steps necessary to be ready. When I was a student, I knew when tests were scheduled, but I usually procrastinated until the last minute and then had to pull an all-nighter to cram for the test. Many studies have demonstrated that learning that way is not really learning – one remembers the information for the test and then immediately forgets it.

You may have heard educator and businessman Dr. Stephen Covey's story about procrastinating on the farm (I had the privilege of being with Dr. Covey on three separate occasions; he was a remarkable man.). He used a hypothetical example of a farmer who planted in the spring and then did nothing until right before harvest time. Then he would fly into action watering, cultivating, weeding, spraying, etc. Can you imagine the effect that would have on the crops? It is absurd! Yet so many of us approach our tasks like that farmer and then wonder why we aren't more successful and/or why we experience so much stress.

One simple way to guard against procrastination and ensure time for helpful preparation is to plan backwards. Suppose you must give an important presentation on October 15th. You determine that you will need at least a week to practice it so that means you need to have a finished product by October 6th. If you would like five days to polish and finalize the product, you will need to complete a strong draft by October 1. You figure you will need fifteen days to write an outline and prepare a solid draft, so you must begin that task by September 15th. If the research will take fifteen days, you must begin it no later than September 1st. That requires that by August, you have reserved chunks of your time throughout September and early October in your calendar to work on the different phases of the presentation. And then you need to track your progress and make course corrections as needed.

Compare the above approach with the way most people tackle such a project. They figure they will have plenty of time in early October to "bang something out" and do not worry about it until then. Inevitably some major problem or challenge comes out of left field that they must deal with and they are in trouble. Can you imagine the kind of stress this creates?

The stress is largely avoidable with good preparation and planning. Effective people prepare and practice. Those who devote insufficient time and attention to preparation are not only less successful, they also experience more stress.

Getting Started

I am a big believer in starting small, building a habit in one area, and then expanding the habit to other areas. So, I suggest that you pick one upcoming project in your life (e.g., a difficult conversation you will be having, a presentation, an important upcoming meeting, etc.). Decide how you are going to accomplish the project, making sure to build in sufficient time to prepare and practice. If the project involves a conversation or presentation, it is helpful to practice it out loud. I guarantee that each time you rehearse, you will notice improvement.

Chapter 15

Become a Champion at Mastering Time

"Until we can manage time, we can manage nothing else."

Peter Drucker

Here is an interesting dilemma: we all know money is finite – there is only so much of it. But we think time is infinite – there are always more days, weeks, and years. Thus, we do not guard our time the way we do our money . . . and we squander it. Yet, time (on earth) eventually runs out.

Various studies show these are the top timewasters:
- Interruptions
- Meetings
- Failure to delegate
- Clutter
- Inability to say no
- Failure to plan properly
- Doing little tasks before important ones.

What are your top timewasters? We are all vulnerable in at least a few areas. One study demonstrated that 25 to 50 percent of people report feeling overwhelmed or burned out at work. My guess is those percentages have risen, not fallen, in recent years. And I suspect that the biggest contributor is the failure to master time management.

Dr. Stephen Covey's Four Quadrants

In his best-selling classic, The Seven Habits of Highly Effective People, Dr. Covey explains that activities fall into one of four quadrants, based on an axis of two variables: *urgency* (those things in front of you, pressing in on you, and demanding your time) and *importance*.

QUADRANT 1: URGENT & IMPORTANT	QUADRANT 2: IMPORTANT BUT NOT URGENT
• Crises • Pressing Problems • Deadline-driven projects, meetings, reports • "Putting out fires"	• Preparation • Crisis prevention • Planning • Relationship building • Exercise and Recreation • Values clarification
QUADRANT 3: URGENT BUT NOT IMPORTANT	QUADRANT 4: NEITHER IMPORTANT NOR URGENT
• Interruptions, some calls • Some mail, some reports • Some meetings • Many proximate, pressing matters • Some of other people's issues • Many popular activities	• Trivia, busywork • Irrelevant calls, mail, email • Time wasters • "Escape" activities • Partying

Quadrant I: Urgent and Important

Most of us spend a lot of time in Quadrant I. This is the crisis quadrant, where one is fighting fires and dealing with deadlines and other critical, pressing matters. Most of us spend too much time here.

Quadrant II: Important but Not Urgent

Most of us do not spend enough time here. We are rarely instructed to spend more time planning, preparing, and building relationships. Our bosses are more likely to ask, *"Is the report done yet?"* or *"Did you fix that problem yet?"* Nearly always, it is the time-driven concerns that motivate our bosses and colleagues.

Quadrant III: Urgent but not Important

Most of us spend a lot of time here. Why? Because these things are right before us and scream for our attention. The phone rings, a person walks into your office, people ask for your help, noncritical meetings are scheduled. Very few things in this quadrant will move the organization – or your effectiveness – forward. Instead, they will consume a disproportionate share of your time.

Quadrant IV: Neither Urgent nor Important

This quadrant encompasses trivial matters, busy work, socializing, etc. Anyone spending too much time here is likely to get fired.

The above is a very brief thumbnail view of the concept that Dr. Covey masterfully explains in his book. The key to time management is:

- Focus on spending more time in Quadrant II.
- Avoid spending much time on Quadrant III tasks.

These quadrants are all interrelated. If you spend more time in Quad II, you will likely begin to shrink the time spent in Quad I. For example, what do you think would happen if the leaders of two units in an organization that are often in conflict took time to meet for an hour or two over lunch to get to know each other and learn about each other's challenges? They would gain a better understanding of the other, which would likely reduce the staff conflicts over time. That would likely decrease the number of Quadrant I fires that each leader would have to address.

Ask yourself: *"What one activity, if I learned to do it superbly well and consistently, would have significant positive results in my professional or personal life?*" I suspect it most likely would fall in Quadrant II: plan more effectively, be better prepared, improve communication with people, take better care of yourself (e.g., exercise, sleep), listen well to loved ones, seize new opportunities, etc. A focus on Quadrant II is the key to effective time management.

So important is this Quadrant II that I added to my executive assistant's annual goals, "*Help Mike spend more time in Quadrant II.*" This is admittedly difficult to measure, but it served as a reminder for her to challenge me appropriately. For example, she would ask, "*Mike, is this CEO-level work you are spending time on right now or should you delegate it?*"

Covey suggests the keys to time management are 1) organizing and executing around priorities, 2) striving to function in Quadrant II, and 3) saying "yes" to Quadrant II activities and "no" to Quadrant III activities. If you will begin working on some of these things, you will be amazed at what happens.

The Clothes Closet Example

Imagine a full clothes closet – sweaters here, shoes there, etc. Because it is full, one cannot add an additional item unless one is removed. Likewise, in our lives, we cannot add a new obligation or activity without removing something or spending less time on it. We all have the same 24 hours in each day. So, to add something new, we must pull time from something else. It could be less sleep, less time with our families, less time worshiping, less time exercising, less time spent on our top priorities, etc. All those are good things and, to me, taking time away from them would likely not be helpful. On the other hand, if making room for something new requires taking time away from watching hours of television each day, aimless perusal of social media, or surfing the web without a specific purpose, the exchange will likely be positive. The point is to understand the trade-off you will be making before saying "yes" to the new activity. Saying "yes" to one thing necessitates saying "no" to something else. Too often, we do not consciously acknowledge this truth. Instead, we simply try to cram more into our 24-hour day, resulting in undue stress and failure to achieve the things that are most important to us.

Two Key Questions

I recommend asking yourself the following two critical questions:
1) Are there better uses for my time than the tasks I have habitually been doing?
2) If so, how might I reduce the time allocated to these lower-priority activities?

Tips for the Workday

The following are several tips that have helped me manage my time more effectively.

1) Block out time when you are typically at your best for the most challenging/important items – and then really focus on them. Minimize distractions.

2) Be sensitive to your body rhythms. Are you a morning person? Then do the "heavy lifting" in the morning. I love the expressions "Do the worst first" or "If you have to swallow a frog, do it first thing in the morning." In other words, tackle the tough things when you are fresh. Otherwise, you will worry about doing them all day and, if other priorities interfere, you may not even get to them.

On the other hand, do you come alive in the mid-afternoon? Then do your most challenging work then. The point is to know when you are typically at your best and plan accordingly.

3) Do it now! Tackle simple, quick tasks as they come up. Do you need a doctor's appointment? Make it now. Do you have an address to add to your contacts file? Do it now. David Allen advocates a "two-minute rule." He suggests if a task will take less than two minutes to accomplish, it will be more efficient to just do it immediately than to write it on one of your lists and track it. According to Allen, postponing simple tasks creates a tidal wave of unfinished items that gathers momentum as it crashes toward you. Reject the fallacy of waiting until you have more time or until things slow down. It will never happen.

4) Avoid multitasking. An array of brain science studies find that multitasking is an illusion. It impedes progress and leads to getting less done. According to productivity consultant, Chris Bailey, "Although pretty much every study has shown that it's disastrous for your productivity, we all strive to do it. Why? Because multitasking feels amazing." Indeed, it does, in the moment. But the science does not lie – multitasking does not exist. Our brains can only do one thing at a time. Much time and focus are lost as we shift our attention from one thing to another in rapid-fire ways. The actual result is less effectiveness and lower productivity.

5) Eliminate time wasters. It is a good idea to track one's time during work hours. I do not mean listing the major things you worked on but writing down what you did minute by minute. For example, "walked into the office at 8:03, returned from getting coffee at 8:12, began work on Amex Project at 8:13, took call from Fred at 8:19, back to Amex Project at 8:27, checked email at 8:44, back to Amex Project at 9:31, etc." If you have the patience to do this for just a week, it will reveal – sometimes shockingly – how you spent your time. Then, you can take action to eliminate the less important tasks that claim so much of your precious time. People who try this are usually quite surprised by the differences between their perception and reality of what the time tracking reveals.

Getting Started

There are quite a few ideas here to consider. Identify <u>one</u> new practice to adopt in your life. For example, you could pick one of the top seven timewasters mentioned in the beginning of this chapter and focus on addressing it. Or you could use the clothes closet example to think very carefully about what you will give up before taking on something new. Or you could block out the first hour of the day to focus on an important task or project before letting the day get away from you. Choose one and stick with it until it becomes an ingrained habit. Only then should you tackle another practice.

Chapter 16

Become a Champion at Delegating

"If you want to do a few small things right, do them yourself. If you want to do great things and make a big impact, learn to delegate."

John C. Maxwell

Learning how to delegate effectively will do wonders to enhance your personal or organizational productivity. Unfortunately, many leaders do not delegate well. Like most skills, delegation is learned through practice.

Benefits of Delegating

First, delegation can save significant time. Teaching someone else to do some of the things you habitually do will open your calendar for other more important activities. The initial investment of additional time required to teach these functions to someone else will pay off down the road.

When I was young, I managed a small restaurant that had a counter and ten stools (no tables). During the lunch hour rush, I worked the grill and churned out hamburgers and the like. When my young staffer Rick asked if he could try the grill, I initially turned him down, convinced that because of my experience, I could do it much faster. He challenged my thinking by acknowledging that he would start more slowly than I would but with practice, perhaps he could become as fast. I finally agreed and before long, Rick worked the grill even faster than I could. This freed me up to oversee all that was happening in the restaurant. This delegation was clearly a win for both of us.

Second, delegation is a great way to develop a person's skills. Learning new skills and gaining experience makes employees more valuable to an organization and improves their job satisfaction. This is one way people develop in their careers.

Third, delegation empowers people. Most of us enjoy the additional responsibility and decision-making authority that comes with delegation. I observed this myself in my later years as a CEO. I began to delegate more responsibilities to my vice presidents, sometimes at their request. After all, they knew their jobs better than I did. The result was that these executives felt more empowered, had greater control over their own areas and were happier with their jobs. The organization thrived. Our members gave all of us the credit, e.g., "*Mike, we love Dan!*" or "*Mike, Shirley is doing a great job!*" Effective delegation on my part enabled us to function more as a team and we all benefitted.

How to Delegate

When delegating, it is essential to be clear about expectations. Spend the time necessary to explain what needs to be done. For example, are you looking for a two-page report or a twenty-page report? When do you need it to be on your desk? Be as clear as possible. Encourage the other person to ask sufficient questions so he or she is fully prepared to take on the assignment or area of work.

Likewise, emphasize the objectives, not the procedures. I love the expression, "*Manage results, not methods.*" Julie Morgenstern, an author and business consultant advises, "*Be clear on the outcome, creative on the path.*" When my board of directors charged me with achieving an objective, it would have been inappropriate had they spelled out the twelve specific steps required to achieve it. I would have told them they are paying me way too much to simply follow directions; what they were paying me for was my creativity. It was up to me to determine how best to accomplish the objective and up to the board to hold me accountable for doing so.

Another wise delegation strategy is to require periodic progress reports. The rule is to check in often enough so that, if the project is seriously off track or behind, you will discover it in time to make a mid-course correction. On the other hand, you want to avoid checking too often for fear of offending or frustrating your staff. No one likes the feeling of the boss always looking over his shoulder.

A great question to ask the person at the time you are assigning the responsibility to her is whether she is overwhelmed by the task. If so, this is a signal to you to take more time with the person explaining your objectives and what you envision it will look like. Similarly, once instructions are given, it is helpful to ask, "What else do you need to get started?" These questions offer opportunities for your staff to be comfortable expressing concerns and asking additional questions.

When I worked for a member of Congress, I was a bit intimidated by him. When he gave me an assignment, my instinct was to depart his presence quickly and figure it out later. This was a big mistake. Had I been willing to stay with him long enough to fully understand what he expected, my life would have been a lot easier. When you accept a new responsibility, your goal is to have a complete understanding of what the delegator wants – size, scope, deadline, etc. The more prepared you are, the better you will do in getting the new assignment done quickly and well.

One challenge for some of us is that we have no one to delegate to. In such circumstances, it is worth thinking about whether you can make a sufficiently strong case for an assistant (or even a reliable volunteer) to help carry some of the load and free you up to focus on higher-level things.

Getting Started

Choose one responsibility you can delegate and one person to whom you will delegate that task. Think through how you are going to communicate with that person. It may be helpful to write out a script that captures all the relevant points you wish to make. Then meet with the person and go through your list. Establish an accountability mechanism and over time, assess how it is working. If changes are needed, make them before your next attempt to delegate. Over time, you will become more and more skilled in this important discipline.

Chapter 17

Become a Champion at Purging

"It's better to have extra time on your hands and extra money in your pocket than extra stuff in your closet."

Joshua Becker

A key ingredient in working and living effectively is to have order among your possessions. This involves consistently throwing or giving away things you no longer need or want – i.e., purging. This habit requires both a clear system and the discipline to do it on a regular basis.

We need order at work and at home and, in fact, everywhere. A logical place to begin is with files and records. Contents should be reviewed on a regular basis and outdated, no longer relevant materials should be discarded. For example, most people have a folder for their homeowners' insurance (if you do not, you should). When we get our annual statement, we pay the premium and then file both the statement and the updated policy document in this folder. In most cases, they join the policy from last year, the year before and so on. Such a practice means our files are overstuffed with both relevant and outdated documents that make our files uninviting and hard to interact with. (See more about this in Chapter 23 on filing.)

How do you solve this problem? The best practice is to set up a schedule to review and clean out these folders on a periodic basis. I do mine every two years. It is amazing how much paper I can discard, and it feels great!

The same principle applies to the piles of "stuff" that accumulate in our offices and our homes. Failure to regularly weed out unnecessary possessions means these piles grow and often distract us, impeding our ability to focus clearly on what we are trying to accomplish. We waste time both looking for the thing we need and trying to find room for the things we want to keep.

The key to developing the discipline of cleaning things out is to tackle one pile at a time. I have found this approach tremendously helpful in my life. It involves taking an incremental approach by breaking projects into manageable, doable chunks. Such an approach can work with anything – sorting one bookshelf at a time, one drawer at a time, one or two file folders at a time.

Once a year, I visit a client (who is also a colleague and friend) in Germany. We spend three days working on his annual work plan and his personal plan. We also evaluate his systems, how well organized he is, etc. One year, I walked into his usually tidy office to find seven large boxes on the floor. He told me that this was stuff that he had previously kept in his house. When I asked why the boxes were still sitting there, he replied that he was waiting for a free day so he could process them. I gently pointed out that such a free day was not likely to show up any time soon (life goes on and our schedules fill up) and asked if I could offer an alternative plan. My suggestion was to tackle one box a week – to block out an hour or two each week on his calendar and take care of that one box. After seven weeks, the boxes would all be gone. I do not know if he followed my advice or not, but when I visited the following year, the boxes were no longer there.

When my wife decided that we needed to clean out our attic (I love her energy), she asked me to go through and throw out most of the contents in my fifteen boxes that had been sitting there for several years. She suggested that we block out an entire Saturday to accomplish this. Ugh! I proposed an alternative. I asked her to give me a due date when she wanted the boxes processed and then promised to have it done by then. She and I each used our preferred method to tackle this task. She spent that Saturday cleaning up her sections. Each week, I blocked out time to go through a box or two.

By the due date, I had gone through every box, thrown away two-thirds of the contents, and repacked the remainder into a few boxes by the due date. She was happy and I was happy. The point is that if a task seems too overwhelming, breaking it into bite-sized chunks is less formidable. Furthermore, it is much easier to find a few minutes or an hour a week than to find an entire Saturday to devote to a project.

At the large nonprofit organization I led for twenty-five years, we began a process of collectively purging. We scheduled an annual Purge Day where all staff were directed not to do regular work but to focus on cleaning out their desks, office closets, and paper and electronic files. We made it fun by deeming these casual dress days, providing pizza for the staff, and designating a team to walk around the office and identify those with the cleanest offices to whom I then presented an award. These practices motivated the staff and created a festive atmosphere. To be a good role model, my practice was to throw everything I was purging into a pile in the center of my office – a pile that was usually quite substantial. Anyone coming by would see the growing pile of junk in the middle of my office and know the boss was fully participating. A lot of work was accomplished on these Purge Days and they ensured our offices stayed relatively clean and up to date.

Getting Started

Make a list of things or areas that need to be cleaned out (closets, records, drawers, files, etc.). Then, pick just one item on your list, break it into manageable chunks and set a block of time to tackle it. Put it on your calendar as an appointment with yourself. Once you have finished that area, choose another item. This incremental approach will result in significant changes. And as your build this habit, you will become more efficient and more motivated as you experience the rewards of being better organized. You will know where everything is, you will find things more efficiently, and the lack of visual and mental clutter will free your mind for higher pursuits.

Chapter 18

Become a Champion at Developing Self-Discipline

"He who ignores discipline comes to poverty and shame."

Proverbs 13:18

Self-discipline is one of the most important personal qualities for assuring long-term success. In his book, Taking the Stairs, Rory Vaden states, *"Of all qualities, self-discipline is one special quality that will guarantee you greater successes, bigger accomplishments, and more fulfilling happiness."* It is critical that one develop the characteristic of self-discipline as early in life as possible.

One of my favorite definitions of self-discipline comes to us from writer and philosopher Elbert Hubbard: *"The ability to make yourself do what you should do, when you should do it, whether you feel like it or not."* Focus on the last clause. The single way to ensure failure in life is to base your actions on feelings. My pastor is of the opinion that boys and girls base their actions on feelings whereas men and women base their actions on what is right. Do you see the difference?

In most situations, making decisions based on our feelings is the last thing we want to do. For example:
- I do not feel like being nice to people today.
- I do not feel like exercising this afternoon.
- I do not feel like doing my homework.
- I do not feel like preparing for this presentation, test, board meeting, etc.

- I do not feel like reading about and learning to become even better at my job skills.
- I do not feel like saving money for the future.

These statements may reflect how you truly feel but allowing them to govern your actions is a prescription for disaster! Instead, we must develop the discipline to do things that over time will make our lives better whether or not we feel like doing them at the time.

Entrepreneur Jim Rohn often repeated this excellent admonition: *"We must suffer from one of two pains: the pain of discipline or the pain of regret."* Rohn points out that we cannot avoid some pain. Sometimes discipline is painful, other times not. But he continues: *"The difference is the pain of discipline weighs ounces while the pain of regret weighs tons."*

There are few things sadder than someone regretting the results of a lack of self-discipline when it is too late to do anything about it. The man who struggles with poor health because he failed to take care of his body. The parents who cannot afford to send their daughter to college because they squandered money on entertainment and travel rather than saving. The person who unhappily stayed at a dead-end job for decades rather than taking the steps to prepare for a better one. And so on.

Jim Rohn says two other things that are simple, yet profound. First, he points out that all disciplines affect one another, with the result that developing discipline in one area enhances discipline in others. For example, some studies have demonstrated a correlation between the simple discipline of making one's bed each morning and more careful eating and spending patterns. Second, Rohn observes: *"Success is nothing more than a few simple disciplines practiced every day."*

The book of Proverbs in the bible is one of the wisdom books and emphasizes the importance of gaining wisdom and understanding. It contains many references to discipline. One need to look no further than the first chapter, in which the author describes his purpose in writing the book:

- Proverbs 1:2 – "for attaining wisdom and *discipline*."
- Proverbs 1:3 – "for acquiring a *disciplined* and prudent life."
- Proverbs 1:7 – ". . . but fools despise wisdom and *discipline*."

Three of my other favorite Proverbs verses also speak of discipline:

- Proverbs 10:17 – "He who heeds *discipline* shows the way to life . . ."
- Proverbs 13:18 – "He who ignores *discipline* comes to poverty and shame . . ."
- Proverbs 23:23 – ". . . get wisdom, *discipline* and understanding."

Some one hundred years ago, Charles Schwab, president of Bethlehem Steel, wanted to increase his own and his team's efficiency. Ivy Lee, a well-known efficiency expert, made a proposition: *"Let me spend fifteen minutes with each of your executives and I'll increase their efficiency and your sales."* When Schwab asked about the cost, Lee told him it would cost nothing, unless it worked. He instructed Schwab to see what happened for three months, at which time he should send Lee a check for whatever his advice was worth.

The following day, Ivy Lee met with Schwab's management executives and directed them to make a list of the six most important things they needed to do the next day before leaving their office for the night and rank them in the order of importance. They were to continue this practice for ninety days. Lee advised them to track their progress by starting with #1 and crossing it off when completed, then go on to #2, and so on. Any priorities that did not get done were to be added to the following day's list.

The executives followed Lee's instructions. Three months later, Schwab studied the results in productivity and accomplishment and was so pleased that he sent Lee a check for $35,000. (At the time, the average worker in the U.S. was being paid $2.00 per day.) Lee's simple advice to the executives to create a discipline of making a priority list every day worked for Bethlehem Steel. It has worked for me and it will work for you.

Another simple discipline I have adopted is to track my progress on developing a new discipline. For example, I have a goal of drinking six cups of green tea a day because of its health benefits. Tracking the number of cups I drink per day motivates me to reach my daily target.

One final thought: in his excellent book, Use Your Brain to Change Your Age, Dr. Daniel Amen cites research that suggests that the most self-disciplined individuals were found to be 89% less likely to develop Alzheimer's disease than their peers. Do you need any more incentive to improve your discipline?

Getting Started

Choose one discipline you want to initiate and focus on it until it becomes a strong habit. Then identify another, and so on. Avoid the mistake of committing to several new disciplines at one time. We are not normally able to successfully tackle more than one new habit at a time. Start small and build from there.

Chapter 19

Become a Champion at Saving and Investing

"Do not save what is left after spending but spend what is left after saving."

Warren Buffet

One of the core skills to be successful in life is to save and invest wisely. Yet so few of us do it well. You have undoubtedly seen the statistics from study after study. Many Americans do not have sufficient savings to go even one month without their paychecks. Very few are preparing adequately for retirement or financial independence.

Your goal should be to have enough saved and invested by a certain age – say 50, 55 or 60 – that you have the freedom to walk away from a job you do not enjoy and do something you find rewarding, whether or not it pays well. You might want to leave a high paying job for one that pays a fraction of what you used to earn. There is power and freedom in having options.

I eventually reached a point that I could financially afford to walk away from my CEO position, and this changed my perspective. It made me better. I was more comfortable speaking up to my board (politely, of course) without fear of retribution than I was in earlier years with a large mortgage and two kids in college. Likewise, I did not "sweat the small stuff" as much but was able to better focus on the important things without fear of distraction. Knowing that you have options really makes a difference in how you approach your work.

How do you get there? There are hundreds of excellent books about this topic and I will not attempt to capture all their ideas. I have distilled a basic set of steps below, each of which could be fleshed out in a whole chapter or even a book.

1. Live within your means. Spend less than you take in. Period. No exceptions. If you cannot afford it, do not buy it. This means if your take home pay (net, after all the deductions are taken from your gross pay) is $2,000 per month, you cannot spend more than that.

2. Develop and use a budget. There are many, many ways to budget. Find one that what works for you and operate on a monthly budget. This will involve tracking your actual spending against the budget to see how you are doing. If you overspend, make a correction quickly.

3. Have an emergency fund. Most experts recommend 3-6 months of expenses set aside for unforeseen events, such as losing one's job, emergency house or car repairs, etc.

4. Never have credit card debt. Interest rates range from 15 to 25 percent or more. A wise rule is that you may only have a credit card if you pay the balance in full every month. If you cannot do that, get rid of the card, and pay in cash. Prioritize paying down the credit card debt you have accumulated.

5. Invest at least 10 percent of your take home pay for your future. I recommend a good no-load (no sales charge) index mutual fund (replicates the entire stock market rather than betting on individual stocks or bonds) but there are many options. And, by "your future," I do not mean saving for a new house, new car, kids' college, etc. Your goal for this investment is to become financially independent.

6. Pay yourself first. After eradicating credit card and other high-interest debt, allocate that 10 percent first before paying any of your other bills or making any other spending decisions. This is crucial! If you are tempted to address any other needs first – no matter how important they seem – you will not achieve your financial goals.

Jim Rohn refers to "two philosophies." One says save first and spend what is left. The other says spend first and save what is left. The first leads to prosperity and financial success while the second leads to being broke and frustrated. Same amount of money – different philosophies.

A note about giving: I made this "pay yourself first" point forty years ago in a speech before the U.S. Senate Toastmasters club, of which I was a member. When I finished, a woman from Texas arose to critique the speech (as we do in Toastmasters). I will never forget it. She said, *"Mike that was a great speech. But there is one thing I would change. You don't pay yourself first, you pay God first."* I could not agree more. For decades, my wife and I have tithed (allocated at least the first 10 percent of our earnings to the Lord and His work. It has proved to be one of the best decisions we ever made. So, you may put aside 20 percent or more of your paycheck – 10 percent to savings and 10 percent to tithe.

7. Never touch your investment fund. These investments are never to be tapped, borrowed from, or depleted in any way. They are for your long-term future. If you want to save for shorter-term items (house, car, college, Christmas, a wedding), start a fund for each of those priorities. But this fund must be allowed to grow. Remember what Albert Einstein said about compound interest being "the greatest invention in human history." Compound interest is what essentially happens to one's investments if they are left untouched to grow. It works like a tiny snowball rolling downhill. As it rolls, it gets larger and larger until it becomes huge. This is what could happen to your investments if you do not deplete them.

Following these simple steps faithfully and consistently will put you on the path to financial independence and freedom. This will reduce your stress and add to your satisfaction in life.

The best seminar I have ever attended was taught by Brian Tracey. In it, he shared the secret of being financially independent: break Parkinson's Law. Nearly everyone agrees that it works but very, very few people have the discipline to implement it.

Years ago, a fellow named Parkinson posited a theory that one's family or individual expenditures always rise to equal (and sometimes exceed) that family's or person's income. Say you started off earning $30,000 annually many years ago and you spent all of it. When your income jumped to $45,000, your spending rose to consume all that increase. Then, when you hit $60,000, the same thing happened. And so on. As you can see, this is a dead-end plan. So, the goal is to break Parkinson's Law.

When your income, for example, rises $10,000 a year, try to keep your spending at the same level and invest the rest for the future. Over time, as your income continues to increase, the amount invested begins to grow. Tracy referred to this as "the wedge." The other strategy is to invest these funds in long-term securities, say a good no-load (no sales charge) stock mutual fund for the future. As mentioned above, this money is never to be touched – not for the kids' college, not for a new home, not for an emergency, etc. The goal of this fund is to make you financially independent.

The key to making this work is to say no to immediate gratification, no to "keeping up with the Jones family," and no to status purchases. If you can do this, you will avoid considerable stress and enjoy the freedom to make decisions that will make you happy rather than being driven by paying your bills. Thomas Corley, a certified financial planner and author of <u>Rich Habits: The Daily Success Habits of Wealthy Individuals</u> notes, "*The most common habit that keeps people from becoming wealthy is increasing one's standard of living to meet one's increased income.*" All the (wealthy) people in his study saved 10 percent or more of their net income every year, and 95 percent saved 20 percent or more of their net income. And they did this before they became rich.

Getting Started

Begin by putting together a budget, showing your income and your spending over several months. Get this information from your checking account, summary of online bill paying and credit card expenditures. To move forward in the right direction, you need to know your current situation today. Then develop a plan to operate within your budget. If you need to cut expenditures, do so. If you cannot immediately save ten percent, save less, and build up to that.

And if you cannot pay off all your credit card debt at once, develop a plan to aggressively get it paid as soon as possible.

SECTION V
Sharpen Your Tools

Chapter 20

Become a Champion at Using Email Effectively

"Email is the biggest time-suck of the modern workday."

Julie Morgenstern

Email is a wonderful tool that when used effectively, saves time and effort, and enhances productivity. However, when not used effectively, it can overwhelm and frustrate us. This chapter offers practical ideas to tame the email monster and bring order out of chaos.

First, the use of email offers significant advantages:
- Saves time: with one message, you communicate with an entire group.
- Reduces confusion by minimizing the potential of one person hearing one thing and another something different; everyone reads the same message.
- Flattens an organization by sharing information with everyone at once.
- Reduces interruptions: unlike a phone call, email can be read and answered at everyone's best time.
- Enhances follow up.
- Keeps a record of communications for reference.

But email also involves disadvantages:
- Risks misunderstandings compared to face-to-face conversations in which tone of voice, facial expressions, and body

language may be taken into consideration. Emails can sound impersonal, terse, and even cold.
- Increases conflict avoidance on issues that ought to be addressed with face-to-face communication.
- Risks spreading conflict beyond the principals who ought to be in the conversation (e.g., sending a snippy email and copying others when an issue should have been resolved between only the two people involved).
- Risks sharing information beyond the people who should be involved (e.g., inadvertently replying all or copying the wrong people).

Despite these risks, email is here to stay. In the rest of this chapter, I want to give you strategies for using it effectively.

Sending Email

1) Keep emails short and to the point to enhance readability. Keep them to one subject. If you include multiple topics, you run the risk that the recipient will respond by addressing some but not all the topics, thus requiring another round of emails.

2) Use the subject line effectively (easier if you stick to one subject). Describe the purpose of the email. Ideally, it will contain sufficient information to allow the recipient to respond effectively. That includes flagging when something needs quick turnaround. Here are some examples of descriptive subject lines:
- Logistics for this weekend's retreat.
- Final draft of policy manual for your review.
- What is the status of the ABC project?
- We need a decision on XYZ proposal by 5:00 today.
- Can you meet at 3 p.m. this afternoon on the budget?
- Power Point presentation attached per your request.

Even better, put the whole message in the subject line. End subject with "EOM," which signifies "End of Message", so recipient knows they do not even need to open the email. For example:
- Budget meeting moved from 2 to 3 p.m. EOM
- Pizza here! Come to conference room. EOM
- Can you meet with Mr. Jones at 3 p.m.? EOM

3) **Copy yourself**: email is a great tool for ensuring follow up. When you request information or delegate or assign work via email, copy yourself so you can easily track of tasks and due dates. Then, if the recipient fails to submit the work on time, you can simply resend the original message with a reminder.

4) **Strive for the right tone:**
- Use person's name in a message to soften it (e.g., "Sally, would you please . . ."").
- Read it again carefully before sending it.
- Think how the other person will feel reading it.
- Have a trusted colleague vet group messages (and sometimes sensitive one-to-one emails), especially if the topic is a bit controversial.

Regarding the right tone, Jocelyn Glei has written an interesting little book on email entitled Unsubscribe. In it, she refers to Daniel Goleman, author of the classic Emotional Intelligence. He discovered something fascinating – people have a natural *negativity bias* toward email. In other words, if the sender feels neutral (neither positive nor negative) about an email, the receiver will likely feel negative about it. Likewise, if the sender feels positive, the receiver most likely will feel neutral. It seems that each email gets downgraded a positivity notch or two. This is good information to consider when composing email.

Replying to Email

1) Be cautious about hitting "reply all." Think first about who would benefit by seeing this reply email. Only copy those who need to know. Conversely, even if someone was not on the original distribution list, include him or her in the reply if they should be "in the know."

I used to belong to a networking group that met periodically. When the chair emailed the group asking who could attend the next meeting, I would always email my reply to him or her directly. There was no need to reply to all the group members because the chair always sent out a list of attendees a few days before the meeting. However, a few members routinely hit "reply all" and copied the entire group. Once this went even further. A member advised all of us that he would miss the meeting because he would be in Rome. Another member responded to him saying *"Have a glass of wine for me,"* and copied all of us. To which the first member replied, *"What kind of wine do you like?"* and copied us all. And so it went. Did I need to see these emails? Of course not.

2) Resist the urge to copy the boss on everything. Some people do this routinely because, *"I want the boss to know everything I'm doing."* No! Especially if the boss is a couple of levels above you. This is counterproductive on two counts. First, the boss does not have the time or interest to keep track of what everyone is doing. Second, by copying your boss on everything, you are inviting him or her to micromanage.

3) Reply promptly. It is important to reply to emails in a reasonable timeframe, at least to acknowledge that you received it. Either reply that you will not have time to get to this email request in time for the sender's request or say that you are busy right now but will respond by a certain day – and then get that item on your next action or to-do list.

This is also a useful strategy for everyday emails that take more time and effort to respond to. For example, perhaps a colleague asks you to put together some information for a major project. Rather than waiting a week or two until you have all the information and then respond, a better approach is to respond immediately with something like, *"Bob, I got your email. It will take about two weeks to assemble what you are requesting. If OK with you, I can get you something by the 15th."* Then add that task to your action list and make sure you follow through. This way, Bob knows that you are working on what he requested rather than wondering if you ever received the email and/or if it got lost in your system.

Processing Email

We are all deluged with email and managing it is a huge challenge. In her book, <u>Never Check Email in the Morning</u>, Julie Morgenstern contends that we interrupt ourselves every five minutes to check our in-boxes, hoping for something more interesting, more fun, or more urgent than whatever we're working on at that moment. This, of course, causes our productivity to plummet. Morgenstern deems email undoubtedly the world's most convenient procrastination device. To counteract this inherent risk, it is important to employ some intentional strategies to keep email from interfering with productivity and focus.

1) Batch your email processing. The first principle is to resist opening emails one by one. Turn off the notification sounds. I am quite disciplined but even I can be seduced by the email arrival sound, thinking, "*Hmm. I wonder who is emailing me. It could be good news.*" Guess what? It is usually not good news! It is usually more work or a distraction from my priorities. Morgenstern puts it this way: "*Email is really nothing but a bunch of interruptions and distractions that appear in your in box without an invitation.*"

Tony Schwartz and Jim Loehr in their book, The Way We're Working Isn't Working, point out that resisting the email's "ping" is akin to ignoring a ringing phone, a fresh chocolate chip cookie, or a crying baby, all requiring significant willpower to resist. I recommend assigning three regular times per day to open and process email – say, at 10 a.m., 2 p.m. and 5 p.m. Unless you are working with a colleague on a time-sensitive project that requires more frequent communication, stick to this schedule. One exception might be doing a two-minute morning scan for any emails that are urgent and important, but only do this if you have the discipline to keep it to two minutes or less.

2) Establish a standard expectation for email processing. Another strategy I recommend is that organizations establish a standard for responding to email, such as within 24 hours. Many businesses have adopted the perspective that employees must be responsive to email 24/7. No! This is a counterproductive idea. Many brain science studies show that there is no such thing as multi-tasking and that our attempts to do so make us less, rather than more efficient. In fact, a London University study found a temporary IQ loss of 10 points in people who constantly checked for email messages during the day. It is shortsighted to require staff to remain in reactive mode throughout the day – and perhaps into the evening – by checking their phones constantly. This practice means employees will not have the bandwidth to think deeply and creatively about challenges and how to solve them.

3) Avoid emails first thing in the morning. Avoid using the first glorious hour of the day to check email. The preferable choice is to use that hour – when most of us are at our freshest and best – to tackle challenging tasks that require our best thinking. This concept is addressed in much greater detail in Morgenstern's book.

4) Unsubscribe from most email lists. Be proactive in unsubscribing from email lists. Resist the thought that it is quicker to delete the emails that come in or you will be deleting them for months and years! It may take a minute to click unsubscribe and follow the (hopefully simple) instructions to get off the list. Adopt a "do it now" philosophy. This will have a significant pay-off in the years to come. On a related note, ask colleagues not to copy you on certain things.

5) Process emails that require a quick reply immediately. If you can process an email within a few minutes, go ahead and get it off your plate. It is more efficient to simply do the task rather than to take time to return to it later. A good rule of thumb is that if the reply will take less time than moving the email to a folder for later, just do it.

Deleting Email

Be rigorous in deleting as many emails as possible. You will never need most emails ever again. Make good use of sub-folders for certain emails needed for reference.

Scanning an email and leaving it in your in-box because it is not as important as other emails at the moment creates double reading, double thinking, and double decision-making (not to mention the nagging it creates in the psyche in the meantime.).

We all tend to keep emails we do not know what to do with in our in-boxes, where they sit and sit and sit, cluttering up our system. One executive I coached who works overseas had this problem. Once when I was in his office, I noticed an email that was a year old still in his in-box. It was from someone who was planning a trip to his country and wanted some tips on what to see and do. A mutual friend referred her to him. A busy executive, he never got around to answering her. I asked him about it, and he asked what he should do. I said, "Delete it!" I explained that the woman had most likely already made the trip and, if he responded now, he would look like a fool. Best to move on at this point. We all have these left-over emails to which we meant to reply, but they never moved up high enough in our priority list to do so.

In his book, <u>Getting Things Done</u>, David Allen establishes a goal, which I have embraced, of getting your in-box to zero every day. It requires disciplined deletion and use of subfolders. He maintains that it requires much less energy to maintain email at zero than at a thousand. Think that's impossible? It can be done. The key is to stop using your email in-box as your to-do list! Many people do this without even realizing it.

I have given presentations on the ideas in Allen's <u>Getting Things Done</u> and coached staff in a variety of organizations on its principles. [Note: I teach many of the ideas from this book but let me be clear: I give all the credit to David Allen and I continually give away his books. His work has really changed my life.] I have heard many times that people feel great when they get their in-boxes to zero. As Allen points out, getting your in-box to zero is of huge value because then your entire inventory is in one place.

Allen offers three valuable tips for achieving an empty in-box at the end of each day:

1) Action Folder: Set up a folder labelled @ACTION to collect all the emails you must act on but do not have time to handle when you first read them. The @ sign ensures the subfolder appears at the top of the alphabetical list of folders. Then record the action on your next action or to-do list (see Chapter 12), noting that the email associated with that task is in your @ACTION folder. For example, write on your next action list: "Email June's budget numbers to Sam (@ACTION)." Referencing @ACTION reminds you that is where Sam's email is stored if you need to refer to it. It is essential that you add each task to your next action or to-do list. Failure to do this means it will be "out of sight, out of mind" and you will likely forget to follow through.

2) Waiting For Folder: Likewise, use @WAITING FOR for items that are owed you (e.g., you ask a colleague for a document, you are awaiting a check from a client or a package from Amazon, etc.). Write these on a separate "Waiting For" list or on your to-do or follow-up list. This folder will prove to be essential for managers waiting for deliverables they have delegated to others.

3) Holding Folder: If your in-box is really flooded and you feel like there is no hope (the worst case I've seen is a dentist I worked with who had over 78,000 emails in her in-box), use a holding strategy. Transfer all emails older than a certain date (e.g., two or three months in the past) to a newly created subfolder labelled "HOLDING." Never look at these emails again unless prompted to do so. Likely, no one is going to contact you about not responding to an email that is more than two or three months old. Then, work down the most recent ones left in the In Box to zero. You will feel great! And as you have time, you can go through that "HOLDING" folder and ruthlessly delete those older emails.

These are a lot of ideas and hopefully some of them will be helpful to you. If you can tame the "email monster," your life will be better for it.

Getting Started

I would suggest that you read through this chapter again and identify one practice you want to adopt, just one, and then be tenacious in sticking to it. Once it becomes a habit – and especially if you can see the value of it – keep doing it and pick a second practice to tackle.

Chapter 21
Become a Champion at Tracking Progress

"If you can't measure it, you can't manage it. Success in any endeavor depends on the ability to evaluate results."

Peter Drucker

It is amazing how many people excel at setting challenging goals and objectives but then do not seem to make much progress achieving them. Why is that? Because they do not keep track of their progress. Even in work situations, it is far too common that supervisors do not hold staff accountable for progress toward objectives.

Just as a habit is simply an idea until it is put into practice, a goal is simply an aspiration unless you (1) develop a clear written objective with a set of action steps to reach it and (2) design a system to keep track of your progress. This accountability approach helps people achieve more than they ever will otherwise.

Simple goals do not require a whole workplan for how to achieve them. But more complex goals require some thinking about what steps are needed to get you from where you are now to where you would like to end up. Regarding a tracking system, I want to emphasize the word "simple." If your tracking system becomes too burdensome, you will not use it. A system could be as simple as a checklist on a piece of paper. Or an Excel or Google Sheet spread sheet. Or notations on a calendar. Or any method that works for you.

One of my ongoing annual goals is to exercise aerobically five times a week and to do strength training twice a week. I have a chart and write down my progress. Many people claim they reach their weekly exercise goals but lose track. It is well-known that memories tend to assume the most optimistic result. In contrast to memory, my chart is updated daily, and it does not lie. In fact, as I write this, I am about two weeks ahead on my aerobic workouts. Of course, you cannot "save up" exercise. But I have two trips overseas later this month and know that I will not be able to exercise much during that stretch. Thus, I am getting ahead now. In effect, I make it a game and I like to win!

Nutrition experts recommend we eat between five and ten servings of vegetables and fruits daily, with the ideal closer to ten. One author recommends keeping a daily chart as an encouragement to eat more fruits and vegetables. What gets measured tends to get done. Keeping track motivates me to get a better score. For the last several years, I have averaged more than seven servings a day. This accountability chart even prompts me to bump up my score after a few low days: I head over to the local grocery store and feast on one of their terrific make-your-own salads. Tracking my consumption of fruits and vegetables has become another game I like to win.

The same methods can be applied to one's work. I once coached an incredibly talented person working for a ministry in Germany who needed help in strengthening his discipline. I suggested that he pick three practices he wanted to do regularly. He chose: 1) spend daily time with the Lord, 2) exercise aerobically at least four times a week, and 3) study German for one hour four days per week. Then I asked him to find some simple mechanism to track progress.

On our next coaching call via Skype about a month later, he reported that he was doing better than expected. I asked him to show me and he held up a monthly calendar. On most days, there was a red dot (for time with the Lord), a blue dot (for exercise) and a green dot (for studying German). What an ingenious way to track his progress! It is simple to do and visually appealing. I suspect that seeing all those dots on his calendar motivated him to achieve these goals.

A great technique I recommend is using a color-coded list. Before meeting with one's board of directors, supervisor, or accountability partner (I'm a big fan of individuals having someone that they give permission to hold them accountable), it is very helpful to use colors to denote the status of one's progress toward agreed upon goals. I use green to indicate the item is completed (success!), blue to designate it is in process (partially done), and yellow to show that it is delayed. You can also use red to show that an item is on hold for some reason. Then, at the meeting, you can celebrate the completed items (and not spend much time on them) and focus on the in-progress and delayed ones. This is a simple system that works well. I have used it many times with organizations tracking progress toward their strategic plan objectives. The color-coded plan becomes an effective management and communication tool.

One of the individuals I coach, an executive in a worldwide ministry, uses this approach successfully. Every few months, we review his strategic plan. As he indicates progress towards each objective, I add the color-coding on my copy. When we finish, I email him the updated color-coded copy and that becomes the basis for our review the next time we talk. This technique works like a charm.

Whether it is a daily checklist, a calendar, a spreadsheet, a color-coded plan, or something entirely different, the key is to find and implement a tracking system that works for you – and then use it. The best-designed tracking system in the world is only effective when it is put into practice.

Getting Started

As with most new habits, the best way to begin is to keep it simple. Follow three steps:
1) Choose one activity/practice you want to do more of or do more consistently (e.g., get more sleep or exercise, get to

work on time, spend at least ten quality minutes with your spouse every day, have lunch with a friend once a week, etc.).
2) Find or create a simple way to keep track of your progress that works for you.
3) Begin recording progress in your system or chart daily or weekly (as appropriate).

That is all there is to it. As you gain mastery of tracking your progress in a single area, you will want to use this approach for additional goals. The tracking system must fit the objective. Some will be simple, others more elaborate. But no system should be burdensome. Simple is always the goal.

Chapter 22

Become a Champion at Using Checklists

"No wise pilot, no matter how great his talent and experience, fails to use his checklist."

Charlie Munger

It is amazing to me how many people angst over routine, repeatable events that happen in their lives each time those events occur. Many of us spend a great deal of time preparing and packing for a vacation and yet forget to take something that we had intended to bring. What is the best way to deal with this? Start using checklists. I have used them for years and this practice has made my life simpler and more organized.

I travel a fair amount, so I have a series of checklists, which makes preparation and packing a cinch. Specifically, I have a Travel – International list, a Travel – Domestic list, and a Packing list. You can imagine what I would put on my Packing list – all the things I want to take with me. But what about the other two? For domestic travel, that list would include such things as arranging for lodging, booking flights or other transportation, developing a budget (if appropriate), canceling delivery of our papers, taking notes from previous visits, selecting reading material, taking a copy of our itinerary, leaving a copy of our itinerary with a family member, etc. Not every one of these items applies to each trip (e.g., if I am on a business trip without my wife, there is no need to cancel the papers since she will be home). But the checklist is a great help when I begin to plan and execute each trip.

For international travel, the list is similar, but also includes some additional items such as alerting my bank(s) that I may use a credit card or ATM overseas, taking the right currency/currencies, packing the correct converter plug, etc. Having these lists saves me untold time and hassle both preparing for the travel and executing it. And, best of all, I rarely forget anything or am caught short by not having something that I really need.

A word about other types of lists. Since the challenge of preparing for Christmas falls largely on my lovely wife, she has a long Christmas list of all the items that she (with my help) has to take care of to prepare for and host our family for Christmas. I also have a list, albeit a shorter one. As a result of these lists, we rarely miss anything important. This approach applies to every significant event that occurs in our lives. For example, we vacation on Cape Cod every summer and thus have our Cape Cod list. These lists reflect the point David Allen (and others) make: our minds are terrible offices. It reduces stress and mistakes by not having to remember everything. Checklists do it far better.

There is no end to the types of lists that would be helpful: keeping track of birthdays, things to buy, year-end to-do's, etc. I also have a couple of yard lists – a general list of yard items to do each year and a specific list of yard items to be done in the spring.

On the professional side, my organization had an annual conference that drew between 2,500 and 3,000 member attendees. We employed five professional meeting planners to organize, plan, and execute this meeting and they did it superbly well. I am sure they relied heavily on checklists. In addition, as CEO, my office had a list of things we were responsible for, such as working with two boards of directors, two trustee committees, preparing and delivering my address, entertaining VIP's, and a host of other items. To do them effectively year after year, I had my checklist (and my Executive Assistant had hers) of over forty items. A month or two before the meeting, I would access the list from the prior year, review it, delete items no longer relevant, add a few new items unique to this year's meeting, print a clean copy, and I had an updated and complete checklist in my hands.

A couple of years ago I read a wonderful book by Dr. Atul Gawande entitled The Checklist Manifesto. Gawande is a surgeon and associate professor at Harvard Medical School. He championed the use of checklists in operating rooms all over the world for the World Health Organization. He makes a strong case that using checklists keeps the best of us from forgetting or overlooking things in the heat of the moment. The simple idea of the checklist reveals the complexity of our lives and how we can deal with it. He argues *"The volume and complexity of knowledge today has exceeded our ability as individuals to properly deliver it to people – consistently, correctly and safely."* Thus, failures continue to plague us in most organized activity including health care, the financial industry, government and so on.

Dr. Gawande describes the incredible effort he and others spearheaded to get medical operating rooms around the world to adopt a checklist before, during and after surgeries with the result that they documented a far lower frequency of errors when checklists were used. One of the six or seven items on the preoperative checklist is that every member of the operating room team – surgeon(s), anesthesiologist, head nurse, etc. – is to introduce himself/herself to the rest of the team. They found that this made the team more comfortable speaking up if anyone noticed a problem.

Dr. Gawande also explains that airline pilots have checklists programmed into their instrument panels so that if a crisis occurs, they just call up the appropriate checklist and follow it. I am sure this simple but critical technique has prevented untold crashes. The types of lists we need for our personal and professional lives are obviously not as critical as the ones described in The Checklist Manifesto, but they serve to make our work and our lives run more smoothly.

The bottom line: using checklists will enhance your effectiveness and make your life simpler. I suggest you get started on your first checklist today.

Getting Started

Choose one type of checklist that would be helpful to you. Then compile it and start using it. As you use it, additional items will come to mind that need to be added to it. As you become comfortable with using this checklist, start a list for another area of your life.

Chapter 23

Become a Champion at Filing

"If filing and storing isn't easy and fast (and even fun!), you'll tend to stack, pile, or digitally accumulate things instead of putting them away appropriately."

David Allen

A good filing system is critical to success. While at first glance, it may not seem particularly important, a functional filing system that is easy to use will pay huge dividends.

In his best-selling book, <u>Getting Things Done</u>, David Allen recommends using a simple alphabetical filing system for all one's files. You may find that useful, or you may prefer to organize your files in another way. The drawers should be less than 75% full. Allen contends that your files will either attract you or repel you and jammed, messy files are a turn-off. I took his advice some years ago and reorganized my files. It was one of the best things I ever did. I used to dread having to go into my files to search for something or to insert a new item into one of the jammed folders. Now, it is a pleasure to open a file drawer, as there is plenty of room in the cabinet and every folder is neatly labeled and in its proper alphabetical place.

The other tip Allen suggests is to use a labeler to keep files organized. This is much simpler than printing labels from my computer or handwriting them. I keep a pack of file folders and my labeler close by and it takes me less than 45 seconds to create a new folder with a cleanly typed heading and pop it into my filing cabinet. When I no longer need a file, I empty the contents and add it back to the pile of file folders. When I need a new folder, I put on a new label for the new topic and it is done.

It is important to think through the logic to creating your filing system. Allen suggests beginning labels with a noun. For example, "Taxes: 2020" rather than "2020 Taxes" and "Travel – Europe" rather than "European Travel." This will ensure all related files are located together under a main topic (e.g., Taxes, Travel). Otherwise, file folders will easily get lost under a year (2019, 2020) or an adjective, e.g., "European."

One more thing piece of naming advice. Avoid names like "Articles," "Issues," "New Policies," "Miscellaneous," "Pending," and the like. They are too general and will be used to accumulate all kinds of things that will become difficult to find if you need them.

David Allen's bottom line is that it is all about retrieval. If your filing system is not fast, functional, and fun, you will resist using it.

Getting Started

Begin by honestly assessing your current filing system. How well is it working for you? If you would rate it an 8 or 9 out of 10, keep using your current system. If not, design a new one. A good first step is to adopt the simple alphabetical filing system mentioned here. Then begin to go through your current files. Clean them out and organize the remaining ones logically with clear headings.

One important note: we increasingly keep our files in digital form. The above advice also applies to computer file systems. Determine structures that work effectively to allow you to file and retrieve all your documents in a simple, logical way.

Chapter 24

Become a Champion at Running Meetings

"Effective meetings don't happen by accident; they happen by design."

Unknown

Nearly everyone has a horror story about badly run meetings they have endured. We have all been there. In fact, it seems that most meetings are poorly managed. This is one reason that I generally resist serving on boards. Few people know how to lead and manage effective meetings. As a result, meetings are often time wasters. The remainder of this chapter outlines some strategies to improve your effectiveness in meetings.

Strategies to Deal with Ineffective and Time-Wasting Meetings

1) Take work with you. If the meeting is a large gathering and you are not required to play a key role, you may be able to sit in the back and work quietly. Of course, you must be careful not to give offense. If, for example, you are scheduled to give a report or address one item on the agenda, it is appropriate to work on other things until the time for that agenda item.

2) Leave early or avoid attending. If the agenda does not include any items that require your involvement, you might ask if you could be excused early or even skip the meeting. For example, you could ask your boss:" Joe, *I've got to finish the XYZ project; would it* be OK if I skipped today's meeting and then check with Sally to see what I missed?"

3) Delegate someone to attend in your place. If your personal attendance is not essential, designate someone to attend in your place. Part of this delegation will involve preparing this person for what might happen during the meeting and how to handle it.

4) Resolve to learn at least two things. If the above options do not apply and you are going to have to sit through the meeting, use the time to your advantage by resolving to learn something. Attentively listening for a couple of useful ideas will change your whole attitude about the meeting.

Advocate Effective Meeting Management

Organizations can learn to run effective meetings. Some of the components below came from a Wall Street Journal article, *"Stop Wasting Everyone's Time,"* by Sue Shellenbarger.

1) Clarify a definite purpose. A meeting must have a definite purpose. If you cannot easily articulate its purpose, do not have the meeting. Period. Avoid vague purposes – be crystal clear about why you are asking people to give up their valuable time.

2) Circulate a written agenda in advance. The agenda should preferably include timeframes for each item. This allows the chair and others to keep the meeting on schedule. While not every agenda item will begin and end on time (nor should it), the group can assess how it is doing after handling several agenda items. This also makes it easier for attendees to determine if the meeting is proceeding on schedule and, if not, to speak up.

3) Select attendees carefully. Avoid inviting too many people. Some subscribe to a "rule of seven" theory that contends that every person beyond seven reduces the likelihood of making good decisions by 10%. Avoid including people from more than two levels of management. Do you really need a supervisor and her subordinate unless both are presenting? Also avoid copying people on the meeting agenda who are not invited.

4) Do not leave anyone out that should be in attendance. Doing so creates all kinds of problems, including potential strained relationships. Decision-makers need to be present or the meeting's agenda will stall.

5) Begin with the most important items. It is amazing how many meetings begin with routine reports and other less critical items. These should be left until the end, if possible. The logic is simple. The best time to discuss and process important items is when the group is fresh.

6) Start and end on time. If the chair waits until all participants arrive, those who are typically prompt will begin to arrive later, thinking, "Bob usually doesn't begin the 10 a.m. meeting until about 10:15. This is a vicious cycle that leads to meetings that start late and are less effective.

7) Limit the duration of the meeting. Some say anything more than 90 minutes reduces the quality of decision-making. Work tends to expand to fit the available time. So, why not try cutting a one-hour weekly meeting to 45 minutes? Or the two-hour staff meeting to an hour? You will likely get as much done in less time. And your colleagues will be grateful.

8) Conclude by reviewing the decisions, assignments, and due dates. The chair or another person can do this. For example, "Kisha will email the group when she has submitted the application; Pablo will research X and email his findings to the group by November 15; Janice will do Y and advise when it has been completed." Those affected should take notes to capture these assignments and due dates. Whenever I chair a meeting, I promptly email either the minutes or a list of action items shortly after the meeting. Having a written record is a great way to ensure accountability and save time in the future dealing with the confusion about who was going to do what.

9) Put all non-agenda items in the "parking lot." Unless these items are so important that the group agrees to add them to the agenda, they should be parked for future consideration. I usually have a flip chart available and simply write all parking lot items so everyone remembers them and can follow up as appropriate.

Getting Started

If you chair meetings, choose several of the items listed above that you would like to implement and try them at your next meeting. See how they work and then adjust as appropriate. For meetings you attend, make suggestions to the chair, and explore whether he/she is open to making some changes. If so (and if he/she concurs) you might ask for a few minutes on the next agenda to suggest these ideas to the group. It never hurts to recommend improvements to make an organization more effective.

Chapter 25

Become a Champion at Using Good Systems

"A bad system will beat a good person every time."

W. Edwards Deming

To be effective and enhance one's success, it is crucial to have and use good systems. As business coach and author Carrie Wilkerson said, *"Systems are not sexy – but they really DO drive everything we do!"*

Take a mental inventory of your current systems for:
- Keeping track of things you want or must do.
- Prioritizing and managing your work in an effective manner.
- Remembering your commitments and obligations.
- Preparing in time for major events in your life.
- Keeping well stocked in all the supplies you regularly use (extra ink cartridges for your printer, paper for printing, stamps, staples, pens and pencils, garden supplies, etc.).
- Preparing for travel and trips.

There are many good systems. The most important attribute is how a given system works for you. Ask yourself, "On a scale of 1-10 (10 being high), how well are my systems working for me?" If you say 8 or 9, you do not have a problem in this area. But, if your rating is below 7, search for a better system.

In Chapter 13, I briefly describe David Allen's effective system for keeping track of everything you have "on your plate." His approach has worked wonders for me, but it may not be right for you. The important thing is to find systems that work for you. The simpler, the better.

To begin, set aside a block of time (a couple of hours) to carefully think through how well your current approach or system is working – or not working – and where improvements are most needed. Then begin investigating other systems or approaches. Ask colleagues and friends what strategies they use. As you do this, approach it like an interview to find out how their systems work and what benefits they enjoy from using them. It may help you to identify the areas where you have determined that you need improvement and see what ideas they offer. Make careful notes and look for themes that point you in a helpful direction.

There are also many good books that describe various systems to help you with organization and time management. You can also glean much helpful advice through online research.

As you investigate systems and strategies used by others, you will likely pick up a few good ideas. Try some on for size for a trial period. If they work, adopt and/or adapt them for your own purposes. It may take some time to find, test and implement the right system or systems but it will be worth it.

If you find yourself getting stuck in finding solutions, you may want to consider engaging an organizational coach who could assess your current systems and offer specific suggestions for you to implement.

Getting Started

Begin by assessing your current systems. Start with one area. Read Chapter 13 for a quick summary of David Allen's phenomenal system. If his system appeals to you, purchase and read the first two chapters of his book, <u>Getting Things Done</u>. That will provide a great overview of his process and the benefits thereof.

Alternately, talk to others or search online for approaches that appear to be helpful for your situation. Try one strategy, evaluate how it is working for you, and add more as you have time.

Committing time and energy to this subject will pay off in significant ways as you implement steps to make your life easier and more successful. When you look back, you will be grateful that you took the time up front to design the best system for you.

SECTION VI
Strengthen Your Relationships

Chapter 26
Become a Champion at Getting and Giving Feedback

"Do not rebuke a mocker or he will hate you; rebuke a wise man and he will love you. Instruct a wise man and he will be wiser still; teach a righteous man and he will add to his learning."

Proverbs 9:8-9

Business consultant Ken Blanchard observes that providing feedback on results is the number one motivator of people. It behooves us all to become excellent at giving – and getting – feedback.

To become better at anything we do, we all need regular and helpful feedback. Unfortunately, most supervisors do not know how to do this well and, thus, either shy away from giving feedback or do it poorly. Neither is helpful. Likewise, most of us do not seek regular feedback from those for whom we work. Our attitude is often "no news is good news." This is very shortsighted.

Giving Feedback

To give effective feedback, the recipient must first have a clear understanding of expectations. The includes both the objectives on which he or she is being evaluated as well as the method and timing of the assessment. Recipients ought to have a written list of annual objectives (see Chapter 11 on goal setting). These are the "whats" – what one has agreed to accomplish in her job. Correctly written objectives are outcome-based so they can readily be determined as completed or not.

The "hows" are also important and need to be clearly stated as well. These may include things like punctuality, effective financial management, working well with others, willingness to be involved in interdepartmental task forces, dependability, etc.

Feedback can be too subjective, focusing disproportionately on the "hows" rather than the accomplishment of agreed-upon objectives. As a result, many operate without a clear set of expectations and metrics on which to give feedback on their performance. With annual written objectives, each person knows if she has accomplished what she committed to do – and if she has, she feels good about herself whether her supervisor tells her so or not. In fact, author and business guru Patrick Lencioni notes that employees who can measure their own progress or contribution develop a greater sense of personal responsibility and satisfaction.

On the other hand, feedback that only focuses on objectives or the "whats" leaves out an important component of how one does his job. If Sam, for example achieves 100% of his objectives but has been a "bull in a china shop", offending others and burning bridges, he is likely someone an employer would not want to keep around. The bottom line: giving both objective and subjective feedback is the ideal.

The seven vice presidents who worked for me had no surprises during their feedback sessions. If they had completed all or most of their annual objectives (and usually, they had), they had no angst about reviewing their performance with me because they knew exactly how well they had done. That is why I believe so strongly in having clear and measurable written objectives and being held accountable for them.

Giving negative feedback is difficult for most people. In her book, <u>Daring Greatly</u>, Brene Brown notes, "*Without feedback, there can be no transformative change.*" She attributes our hesitance about giving feedback to others to two factors:

1) We are not comfortable with hard conversations.

2) We do not know how to give feedback in a way that moves people and processes forward.

Conversations involving giving negative feedback are uncomfortable. Heidi Grant Halvorson in her excellent book, <u>Succeed: How We Can Reach Our Goals</u>, offers several helpful suggestions:
- Speak the truth – tell people what they need to hear. Do not fear bruising feelings.
- Convey that you believe the person can succeed if he or she takes necessary action.
- Be as specific as possible about the problems as well as the steps necessary to resolve it.

When giving positive feedback, praise must be sincere. Even young kids can discern the difference between the participation trophies and those they earned through talent and hard work. Most people can see through such empty words and will not be motivated by them.

Avoid implying that success is all about ability. Praising ability can backfire. If a parent often tells Johnny that he is so smart and then he flunks a key exam, he attributes the failure to his lack of intelligence. He concludes his parents were mistaken. But perhaps the problem was that he should have studied harder. Of course, it is fine to praise talent if you also praise the behaviors that develop that talent.

In general, praise what the person *does*, not what he or she *is*. In other words, praise *behaviors* that are under the person's control. Diligence, work ethic, persistence, a desire to learn, and being well-prepared are all examples of such behaviors. Praising behaviors is far preferable to praising abilities because the latter seem fixed. You want to focus on feedback that motivates. Furthermore, success is nearly always based on a combination of ability and behavior. Top athletes possess tremendous natural ability, but they also train hard, develop those abilities to the greatest extent, and rigorously prepare for each performance. Most coaches would prefer to have someone on the team with less natural ability and an outstanding work ethic than someone who is brilliantly gifted but lazy.

Getting Feedback

In his powerful book, <u>Boundaries for Leaders</u>, Henry Cloud advises, *"To be the best you can be, you must develop a hunger for feedback and see it as one of the best gifts you can get."* According to Cloud, weak leaders are threatened by feedback, while strong leaders embrace feedback, seek to understand it, and put it to use. Even when these leaders disagree with the feedback, they do not become defensive. Instead, they engage in honest inquiry and dialogue to discern the reasons for the gaps between others' perceptions and their own.

In my own life and with those I coach, the following technique has proven to be highly effective in getting feedback that drives transformation. Seek a few minutes with your boss to discuss your work. Watch for an opportunity when the setting and timing are right. Then, tell your boss you would like to get an assessment of how you are doing. Don't just ask the general question, "How am I doing?" or you will likely be told everything is fine. Instead, ask: *"Boss, how am I doing overall on a scale of 1-10 (10 being super)?"* The boss will then give you a number, say a 7. Thank the boss, tell him/her that is immensely helpful, then ask the key question, *"Boss, what would it take for me to get to an 8?"* (Target one or two numbers higher than what the boss first says.) Now you will likely get some actionable feedback. The boss will likely say something like, *"I think you are doing well but if you got more skilled at X, you could be even more effective."* Perfect! Write that down and go to work on enhancing your skills in that area. This approach will give you extremely helpful feedback.

There are a lot of fancy feedback tools out there, some quite elaborate. One popular one is a 360-degree evaluation where the supervisor obtains anonymous feedback from the employee's peers and subordinates in addition to the employee and his/her own feedback. While extremely useful if implemented correctly, using something simpler often makes more sense. And simpler approaches are remarkably effective in obtaining feedback outside of the annual review process. For feedback to be an effective motivator, we need it much more frequently than once a year.

Here is one idea for a simple 360 evaluation. Ask those from whom you want feedback to respond to three simple and open-ended questions:
1) What should I <u>keep</u> doing? (good things that are helpful).
2) What should I <u>stop</u> doing? (things that are not helpful).
3) What should I <u>start</u> doing? (things to enhance one's effectiveness).

Everyone's written comments should go to an independent or trusted person, so it remains anonymous. The trusted person compiles all the comments, and the individual receives the summary.

I did this once to obtain feedback from my eight direct reports. The feedback was sent to a member of my staff whose office in our building was the furthest from mine. She compiled them and gave me the package. I then met with my direct reports and shared the results, and this led to a healthy discussion and to a change in some of my behaviors. For example, I learned I was not proficient at delegating and kept too much on my plate. In response to feedback from several people, I met with my direct reports individually and we agreed on several things that I delegated to them. It was a win for me, for them, and for the organization.

A related approach is to obtain feedback from a group in a single meeting. I recently gathered this kind of input for a CEO from seven of his top people collectively. The CEO explained the process to his senior staff and then left the meeting. It only took about 45 minutes with the group to get the information. I took notes, typed them up and then shared a first draft with the seven. Then I made changes based on their comments and met with the CEO to share the final document. The individual comments of his staff remained anonymous. Fortunately, the CEO was a wise man who genuinely wanted honest feedback. He agreed with most of the comments and took the information to heart. This was a simple but effective process. These kinds of techniques do not need to be overly complicated.

When I was the CEO of an organization, I initiated a simple weekly report entitled, "Good News, Bad News" and asked my seven vice presidents to email me a few bullets every Friday on good, bad, and other things that happened in their areas that week. At first, they balked, finding it tedious. I insisted and after a while they began to appreciate it. They sometimes used it to "toot their own horns" a bit by listing accomplishments and positive happenings (good news) or give me an early warning on any negative happenings (bad news), the latter of which was better to hear from them than from someone else. I could read all seven of these brief reports (each only four or five bullets) in fifteen minutes and have a good understanding of what happened in and to the organization in the week. It was terrific feedback! And, again, quite simple.

Getting Started

The first step is to decide if you want to *get* feedback and from whom, or do you want to *give* feedback and to whom. Once you identify a specific real-life situation in your world, scan the chapter and identify an approach that appeals to you. Or, if you do not see it here, consult a wise colleague who can give you good counsel. When you have settled on your approach, take the time to prepare well for the feedback session. The time you put into preparation for this one session will better arm you for future sessions. Finally, after engaging in the feedback session, do a quick debrief, either by yourself or with a trusted colleague, answering the questions: 1) what went well, 2) what didn't go well, and 3) what can I do better next time. Giving and receiving feedback effectively is a key skill that can be developed over time and will enhance your success in work and in life.

Chapter 27

Become a Champion at Showing Appreciation

"In everything give thanks for this is God's will for you in Christ Jesus."

1 Thessalonians 5:18 (NASB)

One of the main factors that determines whether someone stays in her current job is if she feels appreciated. Some employee surveys rank this far above compensation; yet many managers still believe salary is the bigger motivator. Feeling appreciated and valued is incredibly important. In their excellent book, The Way We're Working Isn't Working, Tony Schwartz and Jim Loehr note, "Perhaps no human need is more neglected in the workplace than to feel valued."

The good news is that making people feel valued and appreciated is easy to do and often costs little or nothing. So why do many supervisors give short shrift to this notion? I believe it is usually because they are too busy and simply do not take the time. This is very shortsighted!

I had to learn this lesson the hard way. In my early years as a CEO of a large non-profit organization, I did not take the time to show appreciation in formal ways. It just did not seem that important when compared to all my responsibilities. But over the years I improved. I began to thank people more frequently, sometimes for no reason. One time at a meeting, I turned to one of my staff and said, "*Sue, thanks for being here.*" She seemed confused and asked, "*What do you mean being here?*" I replied, "*Thanks for being at NTCA (the name of our nonprofit). You could work for a lot of different organizations and I appreciate you being with us."* She smiled and said, *"Well, thank you for thanking me."* I know it would have made my day when I was a mid-level staffer if my CEO told me he was happy I was on his team.

The following are several ways of showing appreciation that I have tried in the organization where I was CEO.

Kudo Awards

To give employees a way to recognize their colleagues, we created a "Kudo Award." It was a simple approach that worked like this:

We designed a simple one-page nomination form (see copy at end of chapter) that required only the employee's name and a one sentence description of why that employee deserved the kudo, signed by the submitting employee and sent to my office.

I signed and personally presented the Kudo Award to the employee at his or her desk and offered him or her a choice of several kinds of Kudos candy bars.

Every so often (usually at the end of a staff meeting), we had a Kudos Drawing. The names of all employees who had received a Kudo Award were put into a hat (those who had received more than one had their names entered for each Kudo Award). A name was drawn, and I handed that employee a crisp $100 bill. If we had an unusually large number of Kudos awarded, we would draw for a second $100 bill.

The staff loved it! The benefits of this approach included:
- Was simple to implement. No bureaucracy.
- Gave employees an easy way to recognize a colleague.
- Created stronger bonds between employees and gratitude towards those who nominated colleagues.
- Recognition from the CEO.

The Kudo Awards were a win for everyone at little time and cost. What's not to like?

Anniversary Notes

Early in my 25-year tenure at NTCA, I began acknowledging each employee's anniversary date. In January of each year, our human resources staff gave me a list of employees by anniversary date. I wrote a short note to each staff member on his or her anniversary date. Most were just one sentence, such as, *"Kisha, congrats on seven years with NTCA! Glad you are here,"* or *"Kevin, congrats on twelve years! I appreciate your work."* This was a bit of a chore since I had to write 175 notes every year but it was well worth it.

I continued these anniversary notes until 2010 when I retired and long, long after nearly all communication became electronic. In the later years, this tiny effort stood out, as it was one of the few personalized, hand-written messages an employee received every year. I found out later that some employees had saved every note for more than twenty years! It is just one more simple idea of ways to make people feel special and appreciated. Tony Schwartz and Jim Loehr are fans: *"As simple as this seems, writing notes of appreciation is one of the basic behaviors we encourage in senior leaders."*

Anniversary Lunches

Another approach we initiated at NTCA was celebration lunches for significant anniversaries. I took every employee to a fancy lunch to celebrate a big anniversary (i.e., 10 years, 15 years, 20 years, and 25 years). My executive assistant arranged the lunches and asked if the staffer had a restaurant preference. Typically, they suggested casual places, but we insisted on high quality restaurants for the occasion.

At first, employees several levels down were not comfortable going to lunch alone with the CEO, so an interim manager would join us. Over the years, that changed, and everyone wanted a one-on-one experience with the CEO. This resulted in great conversations and enabled me to get to know the staff well. For those who were also believers, I thanked the Lord for the meal we were about to enjoy. Interestingly, this was a unique way to honor the long-tenured staff (usually our best people), but it also worked to my advantage because it humanized me.

It also became a friendly contest to see who could order the most expensive lunch. As you can imagine, the staffers were generally reluctant to order too much. I had to urge them have a dessert, coffee, etc. I think the record was about $155 for a lunch for two at Morton's (with no alcohol). . .until Susan came along.

Susan was celebrating her 20th anniversary and we settled into a fancy restaurant in downtown DC of my assistant's choosing. I had the swordfish and Susan had steak; both about $26 on the menu. When the check arrived, the bill was over $300! When I questioned our waiter, he brought over the manager. He explained that while the swordfish was in fact $26, Susan's Kobe steak was $26 . . . per ounce!! After I pointed out that the menu was not clear, the manager offered to halve the bill and I agreed. So, Susan's lunch goes down in the NTCA annals as the most expensive anniversary lunch an employee ever had.

In addition to the lunches, for all staff celebrating 20, 25, or 30 years (and we have had quite a few), we had office-wide celebrations with a special lunch served in our building along with testimonials, salutes, and gifts for the honoree. This too was very well received.

The above are just a few ideas, ranging from the simple and inexpensive to more costly and elaborate approaches. The main point is to emphasize the importance of showing appreciation to those on one's team.

Getting Started

Identify one approach to show appreciation to a work colleague, a family member, or a friend. Pilot it before rolling it out broadly. If it works, keep doing it and over time people will notice and appreciate your efforts.

SAMPLE KUDO AWARD

I hereby nominate <u>Athena P.</u> for a Kudo Award because:

I came to the office on Saturday, October 4. When I arrived, I realized I left my key at home. I called several extensions to try my luck that someone would be in the office. After several unsuccessful attempts, I called Athena on her cell phone. Low and behold, Athena was in the area running errands. She was only four blocks away from the office. I met up with her and she gave me her key to use. Athena saved my day and a trip all the way back to College Park. I cannot say enough of what a lifesaver Athena was that day.
Thanks a million, Athena.

_____   _____
SIGNATURE   DATE

_____   _____
CEO APPROVAL   DATE

Chapter 28

Become a Champion at Communicating

"Your ability to communicate with others will account for fully 85% of your success."

Brian Tracy

Hundreds if not thousands of books have been written on how to communicate effectively. I have read many of them. My intent here is not to summarize everything I have read, but rather to offer a few tips I have gleaned that have worked for me. Most, if not all are likely to be familiar to you. But are you doing them? There is a big difference between knowing and doing.

Wisdom from Scriptures

I get a lot of wisdom and common sense from the Scriptures. The gold standard about communicating comes from Ephesians 4:29: *"Do not let any unwholesome talk come out of your mouth, but only what is helpful for building others up according to their needs, that it may benefit those who listen."*

We are familiar with the advice to "choose your words carefully." All too often I find myself wishing I had not said something or that I had said it a bit differently. Some of my favorite proverbs speak to this challenge:

"Anxiety in a man's heart weighs it down but a good word makes it glad." (Proverbs 12:25 NASB). Be an encourager to others. A good or kind

word, if spoken sincerely, can do a world of good to someone who might be struggling.

"A gentle answer turns away wrath, but a harsh word stirs up anger." (Proverbs 15:1 NASB). Seek to be gentle in responding to others. Sometimes, I respond too quickly without thinking carefully and my words come out with a bit of a harsh tone, even though that was not my intent. The adage of *"Think before you speak"* is true.

"He who gives an answer before he hears; it is folly and shame to him." (Proverbs 18:13 NASB). I am sometimes so eager to respond that I do so before the other person has even finished speaking. This interruption is disrespectful and off-putting to the other person.

Use "I" Statements

One of the best tips I can share is to learn to use "I" statements rather than "You" statements. Our instinct, especially when irritated or frustrated, is to begin our response with "you." This can come across to the other person as an attack. It is far better to keep the focus on yourself. The following chart contains several examples with the preferred wording.

ORIGINAL LANGUAGE	PREFERRED LANGUAGE
You make me mad!	I become frustrated when I see this kind of behavior.
You are late!	I had wanted to begin at 10 a.m. as we agreed.
Your failure to follow up caused the project to fall behind.	I am troubled that the project is now behind schedule.

Do you see the difference? The alternative statements make the same point but increase the chances of having a constructive dialogue.

Avoid "But" and "However" Statements

Many of us use "but" and "however" habitually without any understanding of how much they can hurt our communication. For example, the boss says, "Sally, you make a great point, *but* . . ." or "Pablo, I love your idea; *however*, . . ." The result is that the hearer ignores everything that came before the *"but"* or *"however."* A better alternative is to substitute the word, *"and"* for *"but"* and *"however."* For example, *"Sally, you make a great point and here are a couple of additional thoughts about it."* You are not contradicting the person but rather building on her idea. Consider the example of your boss assigning you a project at the last minute. Rather than saying, *"But then I can't finish the ABC project by Tuesday's deadline,"* say, *"OK, and if I need to do that, what should we do about the ABC project that's due Tuesday?"*

This approach takes practice to become natural, but it is worth the effort.

Say "No" in the Right Way

It is important to be careful how you tell someone no. It makes all the difference. Years ago, I worked for a nonprofit organization as its lobbyist. During a staff meeting with several of us directors and our boss, we discussed different congressional hearings that were coming up later that week. I advised that I was going to cover hearing A and have someone else cover hearing B. When our boss challenged me, I explained why I thought my covering hearing A made sense. She listened to me, looked down and then said, "denied" and we moved on to the next topic. This exchange occurred in front of several of my peers. That is an example of the wrong way to say no! How much better would it have been had she said, *"Mike, I hear you, but I really want you to cover hearing B because …."* and then given her reason. While as my boss, she did not owe me an explanation, had I understood her thinking – even if I disagreed – I would have felt better about the exchange, as would my peers. Her abrupt approach was unhelpful.

Take Time to Explain the Purpose

Another helpful communication strategy is to take the time to explain the larger picture and purpose to others. People are generally more motivated when they grasp the purpose we are trying to achieve because it helps them better understand the importance of their roles.

Once, there were four bricklayers. An observer asked them what they were doing. The first man replied, *"Whatever I'm told."* The second responded somewhat dismissively, *"I'm laying bricks, can't you see?"* The third said, *"We're building a wall."* And the fourth – who understood the big picture – exclaimed excitedly, *"We're building a cathedral."* Do you see the difference? That last bricklayer had a picture of the end result and understood how significant his role was.

The first successful heart transplant was accomplished at Houston Methodist Hospital by the famed Dr. Michael DeBakey.

The employees of the hospital were interviewed later about what role they played in this historic moment. My favorite story was about the janitor. He said, "*Dr. DeBakey and I fix hearts.*" Isn't that beautiful? This low-level employee was fully committed to the mission of the hospital and the surgical team. He understood that he played a key part in the success of the team by keeping the hospital as clean, infection-free, and inviting as possible. It would be transforming if every member of your team had a similar vision. It is up to you to communicate that effectively so your team members can grasp not only the vision but how critical their piece of the action is.

Be Careful About Your Interpretation

The wonderful book, Crucial Conversations, by Kerry Patterson et. al. includes a section entitled "Master Your Stories." It cautions against making assumptions about our interpretation of a situation. We often take the following approach:

1) Observe a behavior. We see or hear something. So far, so good.

2) Tell ourselves a story. Here is where we begin to get into trouble. We add our interpretation (not necessarily the correct one) to the observation and add motive and judgment. Now we are in trouble.

3) Feel. Our body responds with emotion to our story and we begin to get worked up. This is getting dangerous.

4) Act. Our feelings drive us to act based on emotions rather than logic. At this point, things can go badly astray.

The authors share an example of a wife who is paying the monthly bills and comes across a charge for the Cowboy Motel. So far, this is only an observation – a charge for a motel. But then she beings to tell herself this story: "*My husband is cheating on me!*" This story takes on a life of its own, which puts her emotions into overdrive. She gets really worked up. When her husband returns home and asks, "*How was your day, dear?*" she explodes. "*I'll tell you how my day way was, you two-timer,*" she yells, and clobbers him with a broom. In fact, the charge was for dinner at a local Chinese restaurant that – unbeknownst to the couple – was owned by the Cowboy Motel.

The key is to resist making assumptions about stories as if we know the only version supported by the facts. I have had many experiences in my own life when I incorrectly interpreted situations. For example, when a boss was a bit brusque with me, I would interpret that as, "*She doesn't like me.*" Or "*I could get fired.*" I was almost always wrong. Refrain from over-interpreting and making assumptions that may not be valid. It is always wise to ask questions to understand the situation better. Or at the very least to mentally explore other explanations. For example, if my boss is brusque, it may be that she is in a hurry or feeling particularly stressed about a deadline, neither of which have anything to do with me.

Clarify Reality

Related to being careful about our interpretations, it is essential to clarify the reality of a situation. In her terrific book <u>Fierce Conversations,</u> Susan Scott contends that what we believe to be true reflects our own views about reality. But perhaps things have shifted and what we think is the reality of a situation is no longer accurate. To avoid this mistake, Scott advises that one of the first goals in a conversation is to get everyone's reality out on the table so it can be interrogated. She offers some great questions to get a group started:

- What has changed since we last met?
- Where are we succeeding?
- Where are we failing?

We all make assumptions that our views of reality reflect the truth of a situation. However, often others see things differently. Taking time to clarify what the reality truly is can pay dividends and avoid a lot of confusion and frustration.

On a related note, Brian Tracy suggests that leaders have the willingness to say "I don't know" often. He points out that a superior person is concerned about *what* is right, not *who* is right.

Other Tips

Some of us hurt our cause by talking too long or rambling. It pays to be concise. I love Mark Twain's admonition: "*Brevity is the essence of wisdom."* And Proverbs 10:19 says it well: *"When words are many, sin is not absent, but he who holds his tongue is wise."*

Mark McCormack, author of <u>What They Don't Teach You at Harvard Business School</u>, counsels to listen attentively and to really hear what someone is saying. This is helped by noticing your talk/listen ratio. Listening is a critical communication skill and most of us have room for improvement in this area. My wife has been a great help to me in learning to listen better.

One helpful strategy is to not be in a hurry to express an opinion; let others go first. When you understand how others feel before you say anything, it is easier to avoid hurting their feelings. On a related note, if you disagree with something that has been said, do not lead with that opinion. Instead, ask for more information about the points the speaker made that you did not find convincing. Make it clear you are trying to agree but cannot convince yourself yet. You might even go so far as to apologize for not being able to agree. This approach comes across better than bluntly stating your disagreement up front.

Getting Started

Choose just one idea from those mentioned in this chapter and resolve to implement that idea in your life. Introduce accountability by setting up written reminders for yourself (e.g., adding it to your daily to-do list, posting signs around your home or workplace), asking a trusted friend/colleague for feedback on how you are doing, or whatever works for you. Two things should happen. First, the new approach will become a habit. Second, you will likely observe some positive benefits from this change in behavior which will encourage you to try a similar approach with another strategy from this chapter.

Chapter 29

Become a Champion at Clarifying Expectations

"The biggest problem in the workplace is unclear expectations."

Mike Brunner

Most of the challenges we face in our work life and personal life stem from not having agreed-upon expectations. A classic example is marriage. Each spouse brings their own paradigm based on how their parents interacted and assume that is the model for how marriages work (assuming that they come from functional families). Until the couple talks through and agrees on the best way for the two of them to interact, there will be difficulty.

The same is true in the work world. Very few supervisors clarify expectations in writing. Verbal expectations are not as effective because employees often hear things differently than what the supervisor intended to convey. As a result, there is often a lack of clarity about what is expected and how employees will be evaluated.

If I randomly interviewed one hundred people and asked, "How do you think you will do on your annual performance review?" I expect that nearly all of them would say something like, "*I don't know; I hope it will go well. I think my boss likes me.*" In other words, they would have no idea. Not so with the seven vice presidents who reported to me in my nonprofit organization. If they had successfully completed all or most of their agreed-upon annual objectives, they knew exactly how they were going to do in their annual reviews – very well! That was because we agreed in advance on their plan of work for the year, resulting in a set of clear, specific, and measurable objectives with due dates. This is the key.

Many people shy away from committing to what they will accomplish because they fear the hated "A" word. What is it? Accountability! They fear that they will be penalized for failure. It is normal to fear accountability . . . but we all need it. In fact, we can learn to view it as a gift to keep us focused on the right priorities.

There are many ways to set up accountability structures. This is how we did it in my nonprofit organization, but there are variations on this theme that are equally effective.

I required each of my direct reports (the vice presidents) to submit a list of proposed annual objectives. Each one got the chance to write the first draft to enhance his/her ownership of the process. I required objectives to be *SMART* (Specific, Measurable, Achievable (neither too ambitious nor too easy), Realistic, and Time-Based (with due dates)).

I then reviewed them and made some suggested changes.

We then met together – one to one – and agreed on a final product. While I as the supervisor had the final word, my goal was for both of us to feel good about the end result.

We met quarterly to review and discuss progress. The vice presidents usually came to those meetings with progress noted on the document. We occasionally adjusted the objectives but not often. For example, right after 9/11, one vice president reminded me that we had picked up a new significant objective, to develop a business continuity plan in case our business operations were suddenly disrupted by a terrorist incident or natural disaster. She proposed deferring another objective for six months so she could tackle this one and I readily agreed.

Finally, we had our annual performance review. Since we had been meeting regularly throughout the year, there were no surprises. Each of the vice presidents knew exactly where he or she stood.

This is one example. There are many ways to establish and communicate expectations and accountability. The key is having clear expectations.

I have counseled people that if their supervisor has not given them clear, measurable objectives, to prepare their own based on what they think is expected of them. Then, I instruct them to take that document to their supervisor and ask her to review and edit it as she thinks appropriate. I would say something like, *"These proposed objectives are what I think you want me to accomplish in the next year. But I work for you and want to keep you happy so please review these and change them as you wish."* Ideally, this approach will lead to a healthy discussion and result in a final set of objectives. The key is to clarify expectations.

Another approach at the beginning of a year is to ask your boss, *"What would success in the next year look like for me?"* A new employee being hired should also ask this. In that case, it serves as a great way to be crystal clear about the expectations of a position before you accept it. For example, if you think a realistic target is to bring in $20,000 in billings in your first year of employment and the hiring manager thinks that $200,000 is realistic, can you imagine the frustration and angst that will occur if that expectation is not clarified from the beginning?

The bottom line is that getting clarity about expectations will enhance your life.

Getting Started

Identify a situation in your life where some clarity is needed. Perhaps it is a conflict with another person over who does what or a verbal agreement that is not quite clear. If you cannot clarify the expectations by discussing them, try to capture them in writing. Create a draft, share it with the other person, and ask him to review and edit it. Then, you can get together and agree on final language. You will find that both of you (or all of you if there are more than two parties) will appreciate having clarity around what is expected of each person.

Chapter 30

Become a Champion at Networking

"Networking is simply the cultivating of mutually beneficial, give-and-take, win-win relationships. It works best, however, when emphasizing the 'give' part."

Bob Burg

A core skill that is extremely valuable is learning how to network. Most references to networking are in a work context. People are advised to network with colleagues and potential employers in the hopes that this will lead to a different and/or better job. Certainly, this is true. But I contend that networking is an important skill with broad application that can enhance one's whole life.

In essence, networking is staying in touch with people – friends, colleagues, those with similar interests, etc.

Take friends for example. One must work at building and maintaining friendships. It does not happen automatically. The best way to have good friends is to be a good friend. This takes time, thoughtfulness, caring about others and staying in touch with them. I find that, in general, women are often natural networkers. As a result, they are much better than men at making and keeping friends.

Some years ago, I made a concentrated effort to develop good friendships with several other Christian men. It requires intentionality and effort. I arranged a series of lunches with these friends that continue to this day. One man and I had a monthly dinner for years. With another, I enjoy dinner and a movie. Because I have organizational gifts, I initiate most of these meetings, but my friends readily accept and share the costs. Over the years, this investment of time has deepened these friendships, which makes life richer.

When I was young and foolish, I got crossways with my boss and my boss' boss. As a result, they abolished my position, a decision clearly made to get rid of me. (In my experience, most jobs are lost because they are bad fits, rather than because the individual is a bad person.) At the time, I had a desire to move to Washington, D.C. and get involved in government and politics. Fortunately, a fellow staff member in my Denver-based organization worked with folks in Washington and gave me some terrific leads; in addition, he wrote six of them in advance about me. When I arrived in Washington, I visited the chief of staff to then congressman (later Senator) Bill Armstrong. We had a nice chat, but he did not have any available positions. He suggested I see Don Shasteen in Senator Carl Curtis' office. I thanked him and was leaving when he said, *"Tell him I sent you."* I did not think much about that but went over to the other side of the Capital.

I arrived in Senator Curtis' office and asked to see Don Shasteen. The receptionist asked my name and I replied that Mr. Shasteen will not know me but asked her to tell him Bill Cleary had sent me. Shasteen immediately said, *"Send him back."* This is how networking works. Without Cleary's name, I would never have seen Shasteen. We also had a nice chat, but he had nothing to offer me. By now, though, I knew the drill. I asked whom he could send me to, and he mentioned a woman in Congressman Bill Steiger's office. I went there, used Shasteen's name, and got in to see her. She did not have any positions either but told me about an opening for a legislative assistant in Congressman Orval Hansen's office. Fortunately, my colleague in Denver knew the Congressman and arranged an appointment for me. We had a great meeting and Mr. Hansen offered me the job – all because of effective networking.

Some years later, I was honored to be asked to join the Reagan Administration as a legislative officer in the Secretary of

Agriculture's office. Shortly after arriving, I decided to set up an informal networking plan by intentionally scheduling at least one lunch with a colleague each week. In addition to getting to know others at the department, I floated the notion that while I was really pleased to be in my current job, someday I would like to manage a government agency. The reaction was usually underwhelming (e.g., *"Great to hear, please pass the salt."*) Some months later, a colleague named Jim Johnson called me and said, *"Remember when you mentioned wanting to run an agency? There is an opening for the associate administrator (the number two position) at the Farmers Home Administration. I talked to the administrator about you and he wants to meet you."* This was terrific and unexpected news, all thanks to networking. After a three-hour meeting with the administrator, he offered me the job on the spot. He turned out to be one of the best bosses I have ever had.

Most people think of networking as a strategy to get a job. But it is so much more than that. It is a way of life. It is also a two-way street. Building a network can certainly help you with things but, in turn, you can help others in the network. Perhaps today I will be seeking information or help from colleagues, but at another time, one of them will be coming to me for information. That is why networking is so valuable.

When I became a CEO, I joined a networking group, which was invaluable to enhancing my skills and knowledge. I built good relationships (and friendships) with fellow CEO's of nonprofit organizations and we helped each other.

Whether professional or personal, the bottom line is that networking is a way to help others and to be helped by them. It builds community and makes life so much richer.

Getting Started

Identify those with whom you would like to network. Start by making a list of individuals you would like to know better. It could be folks in your workplace, neighborhood, church, etc. Invite them to lunch or coffee one at a time. It may feel a little intimidating to open yourself up like this but if you persevere, you will be rewarded with new and deeper relationships.

Chapter 31

Become a Champion at Conducting Performance Evaluations

"One of the tried-and-true forms of management is feedback."

Dr. Christopher Lee

A significant weakness in many organizations is that employees are not sufficiently helped to grow, develop, and to address deficiencies in their performance. This likely happens more frequently in non-profit and ministry organizations than in for-profit corporations where costs and profits are the bottom line.

Conducting performance reviews is an essential skill. Frequent employee evaluations are crucial to ensure progress is being made. They benefit both the employee and the organization. Ideally, formal written evaluations will be done annually, and informal evaluations should be done quarterly. These interim sessions do not require and extensive written record like the annual evaluation, but there is value in supervisor and staff person meeting formally for this process several times a year.

Evaluations are not punitive or negative. Rather, they are a tool to help employees become even better. We all need to know how we are doing and get feedback on how we can improve.

Evaluations should consist of two parts: the "what" (the objective part) and the "how" (the subjective part). The "what" is about what (no pun intended) the person has or has not accomplished during this period. Of course, this requires that the supervisor and employee have agreed in advance upon a series of goals and objectives. The discussion, then, is around how well the employee has completed these goals and objectives. The "how" is about the way the employee conducted himself or herself while accomplishing the goals and objectives. For example, was he cooperative with his colleagues, did she stay within budget, complete assignments on time, manage her staff well, and set a good example in the workplace? This part is somewhat subjective and depends on the supervisor's observations and input from others in the organization.

When I was CEO of a non-profit organization, I asked my seven vice presidents to provide the following information prior to our face-to-face meetings for their annual evaluations:

- A copy of your goals with your notations indicating whether you have accomplished each of them. Simply write "done", "partially done" or "not done" next to each item goal or objective.
- The three achievements this year of which you are most proud, and which positively impact the organization the most.
- How you have made the organization better, stronger, and more ready to compete.
- A paragraph describing how, in your opinion, you have become even more valuable to the organization. This is not what you have accomplished, but rather what you have learned (skills acquired, knowledge gained, etc.).
- Your biggest disappointment this year in terms of your performance (e.g., an objective not accomplished, a failure that you learned from, a new skill you never found time to learn, etc.). This should be something under your control.

Their answers to these questions informed my evaluation and provided information that I may not have had. I had an opportunity to praise the vice presidents for the significant accomplishments they achieved as well as give feedback for areas of improvement.

If the idea of less intensive quarterly evaluations (all leading to a final annual evaluation) appeals to you, here is one approach:

- Staffer submits to supervisor three business days prior to evaluation 1) Status of goals/objectives (done, partially done, not done), 2) Major accomplishment for the quarter, 3) Biggest challenge/disappointment, and 4) Anything special planned for next quarter.
- Supervisor completes simple one-page evaluation and shares with staffer before they meet or talk.
- Supervisor and staffer review evaluation, accomplishments for quarter, and plans for next quarter.

This process should take no more than one hour for both the supervisor and employee to prepare and conduct whether it is done face-to-face or via phone.

Finally, here are a few supervision tips:

1) Clarify expectations through clear objectives. There is more on this topic elsewhere in this book, but the idea is that making expectations as clear and understandable reduces chances for confusion and miscommunication.

2) Establish high standards and accountability.

3) Ensure effective two-way communication. This requires the supervisor to be a good listener and to give feedback about what she is hearing to be sure her understanding is accurate.

4) Ensure praise is both specific and accurate. Praise for specific accomplishments means more than the general remark about an employee doing a good job. It is also more effective in helping the employee know what they are doing well and motivates them to continue their efforts. People should be praised for a job well done but be sure that things are in fact done well. Do not make the mistake of using praise to be kind or to make someone feel better. Praise must be both sincere and deserved.

With an effective and frequent evaluation process in place, an organization can identify and deal positively with problems sooner rather than later. Never save up concerns to put in someone's annual evaluation months in the future if you can deal with them now.

Getting Started

Set aside some time to think through the kind of performance evaluation process you would like to institute. Review the ideas mentioned above and capture those that appeal to you. Query other organizations about how they do evaluations and gather ideas that impress you. Finally, consult literature on best practices related to your type of organization. Develop an approach and policy for employee evaluations, get feedback from others, and test it on a pilot basis before rolling it out broadly in your organization.

… Chapter 32

Become a Champion at Managing Up

"Managing up is the process of consciously working with your boss to obtain the best possible results for you, your boss, and your organization."

Thomas Zuber and Erika H. James

So much has been written about how to manage people, particularly direct reports and others lower in the organization. There are stacks of books and thoughtful articles with advice on how to do this well, many of which offer wonderful ideas and useful information. Unfortunately, relatively little has been written about managing up – how to manage one's boss and other higher-ups. Yet this skill is critical to a person's success in an organization.

I remember interviewing three internal candidates for a senior position in my non-profit organization some years ago. All three interviewed well, but one stood out because she talked about managing up, i.e., dealing with me as her supervisor, as well as managing down. That impressed me. As a result, she was the one that I promoted, and she did a very competent job.

The following ideas will help you succeed at managing up. Some of these came from an article by George Berkley, author of How to Manage Your Boss.

1) Keep your boss happy. People do not react well when I tell them that their most important function is to keep their boss happy . . . but it is largely true.

2) Learn how your boss likes things done. For example, does she prefer things in writing or delivered orally? Does he like a staffer to present one recommendation or a series of options to choose from (or does it depend on the issue)? If you do not know, find out, and act accordingly.

3) Listen and take notes. Bosses do not like to repeat things so make sure you listen intently and make notes, so you don't forget what she wants, how she wants it, and when she wants it. Remember the old proverb: "The palest ink is more powerful than the best memory."

4) Solve your own problems. Handling your own difficulties will help you develop the skills to work effectively and will raise your value in your boss's eyes. Most managers request, "Don't bring me problems; bring me solutions."

5) Make your boss look good. Point out her strengths to others and promote her. Help him especially in areas where he is not as strong. Sometimes this may mean letting him take credit for something you conceived. Avoid criticizing her to others; this is dangerous and unprofessional.

6) Adhere to the "no surprises" rule. If you learn of something that may embarrass your boss, tell her ahead of time and help prepare her. Never offer new information in a meeting where your boss is present.

7) Become invaluable to your boss. The more you can help your boss to be successful, the more valued you will be. This bodes well for being given additional responsibility, moving up, getting promoted, etc.

8) Create a relationship of trust. Probably the most important: this requires confidence that the direct report will play to the boss's strengths and safeguard his weaknesses.

Management expert Peter Drucker said that the most important thing is *"to accept that managing the boss is the responsibility of the subordinate manager (direct report) and a key – maybe the most important one – to his or her own effectiveness as an executive."*

Getting Started

Begin by carefully watching and listening to your boss to learn everything you can about his preferences and ways of doing things. Then resolve to respond in ways consistent with those preferences. Start with one or two of the ideas above and, once you have those down pat, add a couple more.

SECTION VII

Learn Your Whole Life Long

Chapter 33

Become a Champion at Reading

"Reading is to the mind what exercise is to the body."

Richard Steele

Perhaps the single best way to improve one's skills and/or knowledge of the world and areas of interest is to read. In fact, it is said that two things will make you wiser – the books you read and the people you meet. Reading opens a whole new world up to you and me. In a digital age, it is more challenging to find time today to long-form material. With so much content available electronically – Twitter, Facebook, Instagram, in addition to texts and email – where does one find time to read a serious book?

The statistics on reading in America are concerning:
- In 2019, one-fourth of the adult population had not read even one book in the past year. (Pew Research)
- In 2017, only 19 percent of Americans ages fifteen and older read for pleasure on any given day. The time spent reading (not including school and work reading) declined to 16.8 minutes per day. (Bureau of Labor Statistics)
- One in seven Americans can read only at a "below basic" literacy level – equivalent to a children's book or 1st to 3rd grade – and another 29 percent can only read at a basic level (4th to 6th grade). Only 13 percent could handle complex and

challenging literacy activities. (National Assessment of Adult Literacy)
- The average American adult reads at a 7th grade level. (U.S. Department of Health and Human Services)
- 58% of adults never read a book after high school, including 42% of university graduates. (Brian Tracy)
- According to Pew Research, the median number of books read by American adults is only four per year. But the mean is twelve, meaning that voracious readers really skew the results.

But listen to this: According to Thomas Corley, a certified financial planner, author of <u>Rich Habits: The Daily Success Habits of Wealthy Individuals</u>, *"Ninety-six percent of self-made millionaires read 30 minutes each day for education, career or self-improvement. Fifty percent read history. Seventy-one percent read material that has to do with self-help; 56% read something inspirational. Only 3% read for entertainment. The important thing is that you're educating yourself."*

Warren Buffett attributes his success to the fact that he reads 500 pages per day. *"That's how knowledge works. It builds up, like compound interest. All of you can do it, but I guarantee not many of you will do it."* Bill Gates reportedly reads fifty books per year.

Some years ago, when I completed my annual goal-setting process, I set a goal to read twelve good nonfiction or historical fiction books that year (of course, reading quality fiction is also a worthy goal). Over the years, I increased my total so that now it is twenty-four books per year. I almost always achieve it and I learn a great deal.

Jim Rohn used to say that all leaders are readers, a description supported by multiple interviews and surveys. Can you imagine the benefit to you of reading twelve good books each year – just one a month? Over the next five years, that is sixty books. Do you think those sixty books – in your work, ministry or area of interest or expertise – would make you more capable? Of course!

I encourage you to set a reading goal but begin on the low side. (See Chapter 2 on Mini-Habits.) If you are not an avid reader, begin with one good book per quarter or four per year and work up from there. Ask friends and colleagues you respect for book recommendations and prayerfully consider which ones might be best for you to read. Other good sources for reviews are Goodreads and Amazon.

One practice I routinely use is to underline key points, sentences and sections I want to remember. I often review favorite books by re-reading the highlighted parts. It takes me only a fraction of the time spent on my first reading. I also type up high-impact sections that I foresee using in my work and/or my life. If you use an e-reader, the highlight function does this automatically. Making written notes is a practice I implemented many years ago and it has been extremely helpful to me.

My advice is to turn off the TV, shut off your smart phone, get off social media and read. It will change your life.

Getting Started

Set a goal of reading one good book (quality non-fiction or fiction) each quarter (assuming you are not a reader now). Begin modestly and build up as you routinely accomplish your goal. If you are already someone who enjoys reading, set a goal of a number of pages or minutes per day and work up from there.

Keep a record of the titles of books read and whether they were helpful. Remember what management expert, Peter Drucker said, "What gets measured, gets done."

Chapter 34

Become a Champion at Learning

"The learners will inherit the world; the learned will know a lot about a world that no longer exists."

Zig Ziglar

There is enormous value in knowing history and related subjects so we can take advantage of lessons learned by those who have gone before us. Nevertheless, a key attribute for those of us who want to be successful is to be a continual learner.

In his book, <u>The 10 Distinctions Between Millionaires and the Middle Class</u>, Keith Cameron Smith points out that millionaires are students of life and continually learn from circumstances. They often ask, *"What can I learn from this?"* When tempted to complain, they say something like, *"What is life trying to teach me?"* According to Smith, the key to being a lifelong learner is to study what you love. Likewise, Jim Rohn advises that we should welcome every human experience and see what you can learn from it.

To be clear, I am not talking necessarily about obtaining a college degree, although that could be helpful. Rather, I am referring to growing your skills and knowledge. To be a life-long learner, consider the following questions:
- Are you learning new skills that will make you more valuable in the workplace?
- Are you reading and studying to keep up in your field?

- Are you acquiring the ability to become an excellent communicator with your boss, spouse, friends, etc.?
- Are you learning ways to be wiser in spending your time and your money?
- Are you gaining useful information to live a healthier life?

Your answers to these and similar questions will show you where you are already in a learning mode and where you would do well to focus additional effort.

Self-help author Brian Tracy notes that roughly 85 percent of everything known in a field will be obsolete in five years. Of course, this varies by what field you are talking about, but the bottom line is that the rate of change is accelerating in all fields. It is imperative that we keep up.

There are many ways to become a life-long learner. A primary one is reading. (See Chapter 33 on becoming a champion reader.) Surveys reveal that most people read very little, even in their own fields and areas of expertise. Our distracted digital environment makes it even more challenging to focus.

Another way to learn is to attend seminars or webinars on selected topics of interest. Some last only an hour or two and most will take no more than one day of your time. You can gain all kinds of useful information.

An often underutilized but highly effective approach is to learn from someone who knows more than you. Look around and see which individuals are most successful in your field and find a way to interview them or "pick their brains." Ask for a few minutes of their time and come prepared with specific questions such as:

- What seminars/courses do I need to take?
- What books would you recommend?
- What certifications would be useful to have?

In general, identify wise people and listen to them. The books we read and the people we spend time with will have a profound impact on us.

It is essential to be teachable. I love what Proverbs 4:7-8 says:

*"Wisdom is supreme; therefore, get wisdom.
Though it cost all you have, get understanding.
Esteem her and she will exalt you;
Embrace her and she will honor you."*

Getting Started

1) One simple step to begin is to commit (and write it down as a goal) to reading at least one good book every three months. Keep track and hold yourself accountable. Highlight or take notes on key learning moments as you read.
2) Commit to attending at least one seminar in the next four months where you are likely to learn skills that will help you to become better in your work or your life.
3) Identify one person that you could take out for coffee or lunch to ask them questions and learn from them.

Chapter 35

Become a Champion at Having Mentors

"Mentoring is a brain to pick, an ear to listen, and a push in the right direction."

John Crosby

Studies have consistently shown that those who effectively use mentors are more successful than those who do not. Mentors can be used in a variety of ways, but the idea is that an older (generally speaking, although there are exceptions), wiser person helps a younger person guide his or her career or life. A person may have more than one mentor. For example, a higher-level executive in a firm may help a junior person in that firm. A person more advanced in a particular field may mentor a less advanced person. Or a wise person may help a colleague or friend with a personal issue in their life. The possibilities are endless.

I so wish I had had a mentor or mentors when I was younger, and even when I was relatively early in my 25-year CEO position. We all see things differently and a wise colleague could have helped me to avoid some of the pitfalls I experienced. Everyone could benefit from a mentor of some kind.

The starting point is to determine the type of help from which you could most benefit. Begin looking around to identify potential mentors who might fit your need. Before approaching any of them, make sure you are crystal clear about what kind of mentor you are seeking, and in what ways that person could help you. Once you are prepared, you could begin checking out potential mentors to learn as much as you can about them. Talk to people who know them. If possible, find out if these individuals have mentored others and, if so, talk to one or two of them. Find out if the mentoring relationship was helpful to them and how.

If you are satisfied with what you have learned about one or more potential mentors, think through the best way to approach him or them. If you are not already acquainted, it is best to find someone to introduce the two of you. Once you are face-to-face with a potential mentor, be cognizant of his time and take as little of it as possible. State your case clearly and concisely and let him respond. If he agrees to a mentoring relationship, find out what kind of schedule and ways of connecting would work best for him. For example, in person or by phone? How long for each session? How often? Location? Follow the mentor's lead in setting up the first meeting. One additional thought: if the individual seems reluctant or unsure, you might offer a trial period, say three months, and then reevaluate at that time. This may address someone who may be concerned about making a long-term commitment.

Prepare well for each meeting. Remember, your mentor is doing you a favor, so keep the session focused. Prepare specific questions in advance and provide brief written background information if appropriate. Make notes when your mentor is talking and follow up on most or all suggestions. Nothing is more discouraging than getting ideas and suggestions and ignoring them. Track your time and make sure you arrive and conclude on time (unless your mentor signals that she is fine with extending the session).

Getting Started

Identify an area of your life that would benefit from the counsel of a wise mentor.
1) Determine the kind of mentor you want.
2) Identify and check out potential mentors.
3) Decide how best to approach them.

4) Approach them respectfully and ask them to consider a mentoring relationship.

Chapter 36

Become a Champion at Using Coaching

"Professional coaching is partnering with clients in a thought-provoking and creative process that inspires them to maximize their personal and professional potential."

International Coaching Federation

Having a good coach can be invaluable to your career and to other parts of your life. There are many kinds of coaches. For example, there are executive coaches, business coaches, career coaches, performance coaches, skills coaches, personal or life coaches, and so on. There is no one standard for coaches like there is for Certified Public Accountants (CPAs), as one example. Instead, multiple organizations offer certification programs. Many individuals have effective and professional coaching practices and have never obtained any kind of certification.

Coaching is about helping an individual (or group) to get the results he wants. Coaching differs from teaching, mentoring, or consulting, in that each of those professionals is directive in guiding the individual toward a better or more productive path. In contrast, coaches help the client find her own answers.

The best guidelines describing coaching, in my opinion, come from Co-Active Coaching, by Whitworth, Kimsey-House and Sandahl. They list the following attributes:

- Premise: clients have the answers or can find them; coach does not have the answers, has questions.
- Agenda comes from the client, not the coach.
- Relationship entirely focused on getting results the client wants.
- Two forces combine to create change: action and learning.
- No shame or blame about whatever client does. Coach is confidential and nonjudgmental.
- Real relationship not built on "being nice" but "being real."

In coaching, the coach can make a request and the client can accept, reject, or counter it. Years ago, I coached a man who owned and operated a landscaping company. He had about eighty employees and was working long hours. His twelve direct reports all came to him with problems, but so did many of their direct reports. Accordingly, it was difficult for him to have much of a personal life. One of the first things I requested is that he commit to leaving the office one day a week by a certain time no matter what. He agreed and said he would leave on Thursdays by 6 p.m. He stuck to that and enjoyed getting home at a decent hour rather than eating dinner out by himself in his work clothes. Eventually, he began leaving early other days.

Meanwhile, I helped him to reduce his number of direct reports and to delegate more to others. He was teachable and changed over time, and his staff noticed. One of them observed, "*I don't know what's going on this year but we're as busy as last year yet now everything is calmer and we're getting more done with less effort.*" I knew I had succeeded as his coach when he called me one day to cancel our afternoon coaching call because he wanted to leave at noon to see a Boston Red Sox baseball game.

Every coach does things differently. In many situations, the coach combines pure coaching with various forms of consulting. The people I work with want my advice as well as my challenging them to come up with the answers. My goal is the same: helping the client to get the results she wants.

I continue to be amazed by how many people view their employer hiring a coach for them as a negative. Not so! What the employer is in fact saying is that this employee is valued and worth investing in. When I am asked to work with such people, I stress that an employer providing for a coach is a compliment to the person being coached.

One final thought. I recommend finding a coach who charges on a pay-as-you-go basis rather than insisting that you sign up for a package of 12, 15 or 18 coaching sessions in advance. That way, if you begin and find that the relationship is not a good fit, you are not locked into a long-term, expensive arrangement. That is how I work with people. My premise is that if we do not have a good fit, I sure do not want to waste someone's time or money – nor my own. It must be win-win.

Getting Started

Honestly assess whether there is an area of your life in which a coach could be helpful to you. If so, and if it is related to your work, then approach your supervisor to see if this is something she would support and pay for. Your employer may already have a relationship with a coach. If not, then ask around to find others who have had positive experiences with coaches. The same approach is appropriate if your need is in an area not related to your work. Interview several coaches about their approach and find one that you believe would meet your needs.

CONCLUSION

Whether you read the book straight through or picked among the chapters based on your interest or need, I hope you found it worthwhile. The question, of course, is what are you going to do with these ideas now? The key to any learning is implementing what you have learned. Implementation is everything. At the end of each chapter, there is a short paragraph entitled "Getting Started." Those paragraphs suggest some simple ways to begin implementing these ideas.

If I were doing it, I would make a list of the key ideas I want to incorporate into my life. Then I would prioritize them. Then I would create a simple mini step-by-step plan to implement one or two of them. Please do not try to implement too many at one time. That is unlikely to work. I am a huge fan of starting small and doing a few things well – and then expanding to more things. The key to implementation for most of these ideas is to make them habits. Once you have built a habit, sticking to it becomes much, much easier. But it takes time initially to build the habit – and taking that time is worthwhile.

Let me close with a question from Jim Rohn: *"What are you going to do starting today that makes a difference in how your life works out?"*

I love this quote by Roy T. Bennett in his book, <u>The Light of the Heart</u>: *"Attitude is a choice. Happiness is a choice. Optimism is a choice. Kindness is a choice. Giving is a choice. Respect is a choice. Whatever choice you make makes you. Choose wisely."*

It is time to get started. My best wishes to you as you seek to make your life even better. Go for it!

EXPERTS CITED

Shawn Achor (researcher, author, speaker)
F.M. Alexander (actor)
David Allen (consultant, author)
Daniel Amen (psychiatrist)
Aristotle (Greek philosopher)
Chris Bailey (Canadian author, business consultant)
Joshua Becker (author and philanthropist)
Roy T. Bennett (author)
George Berkley (Irish philosopher)
Ken Blanchard (business consultant)
Brene Brown (author)
Les Brown (author and speaker)
Warren Buffet (investor, businessman, and philanthropist)
Bob Burg (marketing and networking expert)
Jack Canfield (author and motivational speaker)
Henry Cloud (author)
Thomas Corley (financial planner)
Steven Covey (educator and business consultant)
John Crosby (politician)
W. Edwards Deming (professor, engineer, management consultant)
Peter Drucker (author and management consultant)
Charles Duhigg (journalist)
Benjamin Franklin (founding father, statesman, political philosopher)
Atul Gawande (surgeon and author)
Jocelyn Glei (writer)
Johann Wolfgang von Goethe (German writer and statesman)
Daniel Goleman (writer and science journalist)
Stephen Guise (author and entrepreneur)
Heidi Grant Halvorson (psychologist)
Mark Victor Hansen (author and speaker)
Les Hewitt (author and coach)
Elbert Hubbard (writer, artist, and philosopher)

Amber Hurdle (businesswoman and speaker)
Erika H. James (dean of Wharton School of Business)
William James (father of modern psychology)
Joseph Juran (management consultant)
Henry Kimsey-House (coaching expert)
Karen Kimsey-House (coaching expert)
Richard Koch (British author and management consultant)
Jim Kouzes (author and business school professor)
Christopher Lee (human resources practitioner, lecturer, author)
Patrick Lencioni (author and business consultant)
Jim Loehr (psychologist and CEO)
John Malloy (author)
John Maxwell (pastor and author)
Emond Mbiaka (writer)
Mark McCormack (attorney, sports agent, and author)
Julie Morgenstern (business consultant and author)
Charlie Munger (investor, businessman, and philanthropist)
Kerry Patterson (author, businessman, leadership development expert)
Vilfredo Pareto (Italian economist)
Charlie Plumb (U. S. Naval aviator and former P.O.W.)
Barry Posner (business school professor and dean)
Tony Robbins (author, coach, speaker, and philanthropist)
Jim Rohn (entrepreneur, author, speaker)
Phil Sandahl (coaching expert)
Jack Schlegel (strategic planner)
Tony Schwartz (journalist and business book author)
Susan Scott (consultant and coach)
Martin Seligman (psychologist)
Sue Shellenbarger (business columnist and researcher)
Keith Cameron Smith (entrepreneur, author, and motivational speaker)
Richard Steele (Irish writer, playwright, and politician)
Charles Swindoll (pastor and author)
Brian Tracy (motivational speaker and author)
Mark Twain (writer, humorist, entrepreneur, publisher, and lecturer)

Rory Vaden (leadership speaker and author)
Rick Warren (pastor and author)
Laura Whitworth (coaching expert)
Carrie Wilkerson (business coach and author)
Stephanie Winston (author and organizational consultant)
Zig Ziglar (author, motivational speaker)
Thomas Zuber (physician and medical school professor)

ABOUT THE AUTHOR

Michael E. Brunner is the president and founder of Brunner & Associates, Inc., a consulting firm specializing in helping organizations and individuals with strategic planning, coaching, facilitation, and other organizational and management issues. The firm focuses on small businesses, non-profit organizations, and ministries.

Mr. Brunner honed his leadership and management expertise during over thirty years with trade associations and the public sector. He served as CEO of the National Telecommunications Cooperative Association (NTCA), a large, national trade association representing the special needs of America's small, rural telephone systems. He also headed its subsidiary corporation, the Services Management Corporation. He directed congressional relations for the American Meat Institute, the national trade association of the meat packing industry.

His public sector experience includes serving in the U. S. Department of Agriculture as the associate administrator for the Farmers Home Administration and as a legislative officer, as well as on the legislative staffs of two U.S. congressmen. He has also served as an elected public official on both the Arlington County Board and the Arlington County School Board and chaired the Arlington County Employee Retirement Board.

Mr. Brunner has volunteered as a coach and consultant with Young Life, a worldwide ministry in over one hundred countries.

Mr. Brunner earned both his B.S. and M.B.A. degrees from Bowling Green State University as well as a master's degree in public administration from George Washington University. He is a certified public accountant and a certified financial planner.

He currently lives in Arlington, Virginia with his wife, Elizabeth.